RICK MINTER

MASCOTS
FOOTBALL'S FURRY FRIENDS

Filbert Fox, Welford and JT the Tigers, Whaddney the
Robin, Sammy the Stag, Mr and Mrs Magpie, and Dennis
welcome punters to a community day at Leicester in 2003.

RICK MINTER

MASCOTS
FOOTBALL'S FURRY FRIENDS

TEMPUS

The author meets a celebrity lion.

First published 2004

Tempus Publishing Limited
The Mill, Brimscombe Port,
Stroud, Gloucestershire, GL5 2QG
www.tempus-publishing.com

British Library Cataloguing in Publication Data.
A catalogue record for this book is available from the British Library.

ISBN 0 7524 3179 X

Typesetting and origination by Tempus Publishing Limited.
Printed in Great Britain.

CONTENTS

PREFACE 6

CHARACTER POWER – START BELIEVING 7

THE MASCOT EXPLAINED 9

GOLDEN OLDIES 12

THE A-Z OF ENGLISH CLUB MASCOTS 15

CREATURES FROM THE DEPTHS 111

SCOTLAND'S BEASTIE BOYS 121

MEET YOUR MAKER 133

MASCOTS BEHAVING BADLY 137

YOUR COUNTRY NEEDS YOU 138

INSIDE OUT – LIFE AS A MASCOT 141

A STAGGERING SIGHT – THE MASCOT GRAND NATIONAL 154

PREFACE

It was my father who opened my eyes to mascots. I was at Leicester's Filbert Street, not even aware of Filbert Fox doing his stuff right before me. 'Brilliant mascot!' said dad. I stopped checking the team sheets and gazed at the scene. I was struck by the effort Filbert went to in making people's day, and the contented faces of children and parents.

My dad's work as an artist, and in making characters for plays and for carnivals, made a big impression on me as I grew up. On many mornings I'd sit down to breakfast next to a spectacular creature's head, crafted from papier mâché, drying out on the kitchen boiler – the product of Dad's late-night task for a local charity, normally for nothing.

From that moment at Filbert Street I was reminded of those characters of my childhood, and I stopped taking mascots for granted. Then the chance to help create a mascot for my local club, Cheltenham Town, was too good to miss. I learnt what it takes to make it all happen – both the hassle and the fun involved in getting a mascot ready for its work: in Cheltenham's case, a giant robin, Whaddney.

I often carry Whaddney's sweet bucket and see the character and the crowd as they mix – the jokes and laughter are all very real, as people get close to something connected to their club. The visiting fans feel valued too, because they've been greeted and given a chance to strike up some banter. Finally, through Whaddney, I've met many of the other mascots – the standard bearers for their clubs. The colourful world they create is a vital way of connecting clubs to their supporters and communities. I hope this book shows some of it.

FURRY THANKS...

In putting this book together there are dozens of people to thank, especially all the mascots and the people who help them at their clubs, their supporters' clubs, their local papers, and in their families – I hope it's been worth it. Other people need special thanks for their wise advice and their encouragement. Thanks to all of you for helping it along:

James Howarth, Ian Clifford, Barry Wood, Angela Hallam, David Scott, Chris and Michael Butler, Jim Allen, Stephen Martin, Lenny Berry, Alex Bedingham, Gary Linke, Ken Robertson, Phil Drew, John Kirk, Simon Burnton, Cheltenham Town FC and its terrific fans, and Whaddney. Finally, thanks to my dad, Guy Minter, and my own support team of Ellie, Natalie, and Owen, all of whom have helped beyond the call even of family duty.

The help of the following photograhers and illustrators is much appreciated:
Empics and Action Images for a quota of the photos in the book. *South Wales Evening Post* for the back cover photo of Cyril. Front cover photo by Rick Minter, from Mascot Grand National, Huntingdon, 2003. Other cover images courtesy of Manchester Utd, Swindon Town and Two Can Design. A proportion of this book's royalties will go to a fund for mascots' expenses when they help at their national events for charity. Dave Green (page 4 photo).

Welcome to mascot world

At last, mascots have their own book, for their own amazing tales. This book explains their origins, their quirks, and their finest moments.

Whatever mood we're in, whatever our club's highs and lows, mascots cheer us up – from Arsenal's Gunnersaurus to Yeovil's Jolly Green Giant, from Elvis with his jellied-eel ears at Southend to Nutz, the squirrel with the massive blue bushy tail at Kilmarnock. All these characters are kind and funny, and, in case you couldn't guess, they're scheming and artful too! But most of all they're the proud symbols of our clubs – they keep us smiling and lift our spirits.

In this book you can...

Find out what mascots do for their clubs, their communities, and their fans. Most of them can't talk, but they have still given interviews, in their own body language, to tell us their stories.

Re-live legendary mascot moments – heroic deeds, embarrassing moments, squabbles, and even tales of love, jealousy and revenge. No wonder some mascots are now household names.

Go behind the scenes at great events like the Mascot Grand National, and at mascots' own matches. The drama and the plotting is unreal!

Why mascots matter...

The club and its fans...

Mascots make a link to the communities served by their clubs. They represent the supporters as much as the club, and they show that the roots of football can be colourful and glamorous too.

The symbol comes to life...

We all care about the symbols, nicknames and legends of our club – mascots make them real again. They are a bit of our club that we can reach out and touch.

Someone to lean on...
Dunfermline's Sammy the Tammy finds a friend.

Christmas Robin: Cheltenham's Whaddney
in festive spirit at Whaddon Road.

CHARACTER POWER
START BELIEVING

The clown and the jester...

Mascots are a live comedy act. They gee us up and stir our emotions. They have no rules, so what pranks will they play, and where will they draw the line? We want them to be cool as well as cuddly, and naughty as well as innocent. This book shows how they do it – how they mix fur and attitude!

Out in front...

Mascots might visit when we're feeling down in hospital, they might join in the carnival, open a school fête, and switch on Christmas lights with Santa. They rev us up before kick off, they show the goalscorer how to party, and they can even help their club in a time of crisis.

Being together...

Having mascots around, watching them be a hero or playing the fool, can help us pull together. They make us feel part of something, so we can all cheer, sing, or laugh together. Thank you mascots, for brightening up our national game. This book is a tribute to your part of football's folklore.

Wild life – Preston fans and Deepdale in play-off mood in 2001.

PS: A handful of football clubs don't appear in the book as they didn't have a mascot when it was prepared in 2003. Here's what they're missing...

Thanks to: Dunfermline Press, Andrew Leathley, York City, Lancashire Evening Post.

Fans to the rescue – Yorkie the Lion is joined by neighbours City Gent from Bradford City (right) and Man City's Moonchester (left) as the York City Supporters' Trust takes to the streets during its bid to save the club.

Dictionaries define the word mascot like this...

Mascot

A person, animal, or object adopted by a group as a symbol especially to bring them good luck. From the French 'mascotte', from 'masco' witch, magician, charm, which comes from Medieval Latin 'masca' meaning witch and spectre.

Jingles on the Jester – Devilstick Pete with his lucky charm – a ferret skin! Pete can still be seen juggling and acting the fool at Medieval fares and civil war battle re-enactments across England.

So are mascots really descended from witches and magicians, people who carried charms and cast spells – both lucky and not so lucky? No mascots admitted to casting spells when they gave us their stories for this book. But supporters have always carried or worn lucky charms and personal mascots, like pendants, teddies and monkeys in club colours, and badges, special coins, and even lucky pants! So perhaps there is indeed a link with the original French *Mascotte* from the 1850s. And, wait for it, the word 'charm' comes from the latin *carmen*, a chant. Does that make anyone who sings at a match a mascot?

Totems

Signs and pictures of animals, birds and beasts can be seen on totem poles and cave paintings in some ancient races – this is a way of honouring the creature that the group or tribe is connected with, because of a dependence on it for food, or because the animal is a god associated with the land, sea or sky in the area. People of high status in some tribes even wore the skin of the animal they revered. Totems are also symbols on shields, flags and standards which connect a family or clan with the symbolised creature.

Sign him up – A Hereford bull is paraded around Hereford United's Edgar Street before a 1996 FA Cup tie against Tottenham. In 1948 the club's badge introduced a Hereford Bull after the world-famous breed of Hereford cattle, and the club later adopted the nickname of 'the Bulls'.

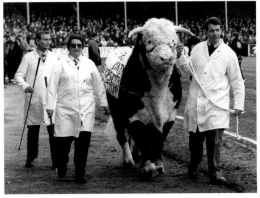

THE MASCOT EXPLAINED

Monkey joins the party – a Yeovil supporter's monkey mascot joins the celebration, as Yeovil win the Conference and join the Football League in 2003 for the first time in their history.

Fools, jesters and clowns

The statue heads and gargoyles pulling faces on churches were the medieval stonemasons' way of poking fun, and of representing the fools of the time. From medieval times to the reign of Charles I, there are records of fools and jesters working as entertainers in wealthy households. They had licence to use bawdy behaviour, and could joke and mock. They were the satirists of their day, and could speak out against the ruler's ideas without punishment. Jesters and fools can even be traced back to the Egyptian pharaohs, who employed Pygmies as dancers and buffoons, and to the courts of Chinese emperors well before the time of Christ. Clowns have evolved by doing set routines and acts, rather than the jester's improvised jokes and satire. Clowns can be traced to ancient Greece where comic actors would mock the actions of serious characters in mimes and plays of the time. Clowns also appeared in Roman times, when the characteristic pointed hat and bright robe came about. The first circus clown appeared in England in 1805, although travelling minstrels and entertainers used comic actors in the late Middle Ages to imitate the antics of court jesters.

Standard Bearers

Coats of arms and royal standards were held aloft in flags and displayed outside the leader's tent at times of battle for troops and supporters to rally behind. Seizing the opponents' standard was an important act, and could demoralise their army.

Heraldry, club crests and mascots

The symbols in medieval heraldry were used in warfare on flags, shields and coats of arms so armies could spot friend and foe – recognising a coat of arms was crucial in the heat of a battle. Many mascots come from a symbol on their club's crest, and many of the crests come from the Coat of Arms of their town. The lion is the most important and regal of the animals used in heraldry. As king of the beasts the lion was believed to be a sign of strength and power, and so was popular in heraldic devices. It's no surprise that there are plenty of lions and several Roarys amongst the mascots. The lion may be king of the beasts, but in heraldry and in fables it has no control over birds – something that's not lost on Cyril the Swan! Eagles in heraldry were signs of imperial power, as illustrated in the arms of the Roman town of Colchester, where mascot Eddie the Eagle takes on the cause today for Colchester Utd. His counterparts, Pete and Alice, display the Eagle's might at Crystal Palace.

Four legs and real fur

There is a long tradition of using mascots in military regiments, with creatures ranging from goats to penguins parading with their troops. Four-legged mascots that can still be seen at clubs today on occasions include Private Derby the Ram at Derby County and Hereford United's bull. Using real mascots can be messy though!

Thanks to: *A Dictionary of English Folklore*, by Jacqueline Simpson and Steve Round (Oxford University Press); *Encyclopaedia Britannica*; *Heraldry*, by Ottfried Neubecker (MacDonald & James), Richard Prime (Hereford Utd info), *The Hereford Times* (Hereford Bull photo).

GOLDEN OLDIES
20TH CENTURY FUR, FLESH AND FOXES

The recent trend of furry mascots started with Crystal Palace's Pete the Eagle, Chelsea's Stamford, Villa's Hercules, Wolves' Wolfie, and Leicester's Filbert Fox. Most of these critters made their debuts in the late 1980s and early '90s, and all have had plastic surgery since. Most clubs were quick to follow the trend, and mascots arrived at other stadiums through the 1990s.

The olden days...

There have been previous generations of mascots – they were few and far between, and must have yearned for friends to take penalties with, but they stalked the touchline and welcomed the fans, just like their offspring today. The clubs to have had them include Barnsley, who used Amos, a midget who rode the club's mascot donkey in 1910; Millwall, who had a furry lion in the 1920s; and Leicester, who had a fox character, complete with bowler hat and stick, in the 1940s. Ogdens cigarettes produced a fascinating set of 52 illustrated cards of club mascot pictures in 1933. Some,

like the Derby ram and Sunderland black cat are uncannily similar to today's character, others, such as the undertaker of Bury or the citizen of Manchester City, are radically different. Liverpool, without a mascot today, were represented by a mariner.

From 1902 to 1905 Manchester United had a St Bernard dog called 'The Major'. He was followed by Billy, a real goat, who died in 1909 after reputedly getting drunk after celebrating United's 1909 FA Cup success. United had several individuals who acted as mascots through the following decades, the most famous being Jack Irons in the 1940s and '50s. He carried a red and white umbrella and wore club colours on his top hat and tails.

Real people and their rituals

Peterborough Utd promoted their nickname through Mr Posh, introduced in 1934, and David Arthur was a young lad who represented Bolton Wanderers home

On the prowl in Millwall – a four legged lion, or has he slipped up? Millwall run out with their lion, and a young mascot on the right, in 1927.

and away in the 1950s. Rituals amongst crowds included Cardiff supporters putting leeks on the centre spot before games in the 1950s, and a Carlisle mascot who placed a stuffed fox on the centre spot before games in the '60s to mark the area's links with celebrated huntsman John Peel. Foxy, the club's present furry character, keeps the connection going today.

The Pompey Sailor

Portsmouth are steeped in a special mascot tradition that reflects the town's strong links with the Navy. Just after the Second World War, a former sailor dressed up in Naval rig paraded a board around the ground with the team changes on. From 1952 to 1973 his successor Barry Harris dressed in a full white sailor's outfit and wore over 40 lapel badges of different football clubs. He threw sweets to the crowd, encouraged them to sing, and sometimes got a toilet roll thrown back at him! The current Pompey Sailor appears in navy blue rig with navy coat and carries a wooden board with the club's 'Play up Pompey' chant. The Sailor Mascot's cartoon has appeared for over 50 years on the Saturday night sports paper with a thumbs-up smile if Pompey have won, a blank look if they've drawn, and a droopy mouth if they've lost.

Toffees anyone?

Everton's Toffeemen nickname came about through links with two local toffee shops associated with the early years of Everton. Mother Noblett's Toffee Shop invented Everton Mints in the 1890s. They were liked by Everton supporters because the black and white stripes resembled an old Everton strip. But the rival Everton Toffee Shop wasn't to be outdone, and its owner, Old Ma Bushell, got the club's permission for her grand daughter, Jemima, to hand out Everton Toffees to supporters in the ground before kick-off. Generations of toffee ladies have since dressed up like Jemima and scattered toffees to the crowd from their basket. Today,

Grooming the cockerel – the Tottenham cockerel stands proud while removed from his perch, as White Hart Lane gets a new stand in 1934. Chirpy brings the cockerel to life at the stadium today.

Toffees for Liverpool? The Everton Toffee Lady watches Liverpool emerge for a 1960s derby at Goodison Park.

GOLDEN OLDIES
20TH CENTURY FUR, FLESH AND FOXES

girls from the Junior Supporters Club have the honour of being toffee lady for the day, and continuing one of football's oldest mascot traditions. The original Toffee Lady is pictured on the local *Football Echo* newspaper – crying if Everton lose, but dancing a jig if they've won!

Thanks to: Mark Wylie (Man Utd info), Richard Owen and Barry Harris (Portsmouth info), *Liverpool Evening Echo* (Toffee Lady photo); Everton FC (Toffee Lady), R. Wesley and Getty Images (cockerel photo), H.F. Davis and Getty Images (Millwall lion photo).

right: English pride – The late Ken Bailey on tour with England in 1976. Ken was a faithful mascot at his local AFC Bournemouth and he accompanied England home and away from the 1960s to the 1980s. In 1969 Subbuteo produced a table football character of Ken in his England mascot colours.

below: Posh Geordies! Peterborough Utd's Mr Posh conducts the Newcastle supporters in full voice at Peterborough's London Road. Mr Posh started life in 1934 and seven people have filled his shoes during that time.

THE A – Z OF ENGLISH CLUB MASCOTS

Jurassic Fur

Legend has it that Gunnersaurus came from a dinosaur egg unearthed during excavation work at Highbury in 1993. Gunnersaurus hatched out and was asked to lead the Junior Gunners' Club. The cannon on the club crest just wouldn't work as a furry character, so Gunner was offered the top job as mascot too!

'Who are ya?'
GUNNERSAURUS

Age
I was hatched in 1993 but my egg lasted over 145 million years from the Jurassic period!

What's your trademark?
Mind my tail when I change direction!

How do you take penalties?
I take a big run up with my head down and eyes closed. I then stop, give it a big hoof and hope it works. It's not easy when you're feet are even bigger than Patrick Vieira's!

Interests outside football?
When I'm not fitness training I like watching the Flintstones!

Finest hour
I had a great time skidding around at the 'mascots on ice' game at London Arena. I played net minder and laid on my side so my huge belly covered the whole ice hockey goal – it worked a treat and the ball just bounced off me every time. Perhaps I should call up a big brother to do the same at Highbury!

Best mate
Former Arsenal goalkeeper and England legend David Seaman – I gave him a hug before every kick-off to calm his nerves.

Favourite food
I'm a herbivore, so I only eat vegetables, grass and shrubs. It helps keep the grass down at Highbury and the groundsman pays me back in chips.

Millennium dino – Gunner warms up at the FA Cup final.

ARSENAL
GUNNERSAURUS

Highlights of your career...
I had a brilliant time meeting the fans at Lens before our European Cup tie there. It was difficult to mime in French though!

Best thing about mascot life...
I help with our awards at Highbury for brave and deserving kids each year. And nothing beats pulling on the red and white shirt – it always sends a tingle down my scales!

Thanks to: Sue Connelly, Stuart MacFarlane, Andy Exley. Empics.

right: On parade – Gunner inspects a member of his fan club.

Worms eye view… Farnborough Town's Boro Bug tries to separate Ian Wright and Gunner.

Lions on the loose

Scotsman William McGregor formed Aston Villa in 1874. He left his mark by including the Scottish lion centre-stage on the club crest. Today, Hercules and Bella are the mighty standard bearers of the club, but it's the English lionheart that they promote as they look after the faithful villans.

'Who are ya?'
HERCULES

Highlights of your career
Starring in the Disney Channel Mascot Cup – I showed 'em how a lion can pounce in goal.

Finest hour
Leading out the team at the Wembley 2000 Cup Final, even though we lost to another lion – Chelsea's Stamford.

Favourite food
Gazelle, chips and beans.

Worst thing about mascot life...
The heat of the jungle – you'd think I'd have acclimatised by now!

Best thing about mascot life...
I'll go anywhere and see anyone to help out my part of the Spaghetti Junction jungle.

'Who are ya?'
BELLA

What's your trademark?
My ability to tame Hercules.

Interests outside football?
Visiting safari parks and shopping.

Lion love! Hercules and Bella were married at Villa Park in 2000, as part of Aston Villa's 125th anniversary. The event even featured on BBC's *Match of The Day*.

ASTON VILLA
HERCULES AND BELLA

Finest hour
Marrying Herc on the pitch. How many people get tens of thousands at their wedding and then have it watched on telly by millions?

Worst thing about mascot life...
Sometimes the grass gets in my claws so I keep my gloves on.

Best thing about mascot life...
Seeing all the footballers' legs... okay, okay, meeting all the lovely fans and waving like the Queen – she copied the style from me!

Thanks to: Tina Cole and Aston Villa FC.

Safe paws – Hercules at the Disney channel Mascot Cup.

Every dog has his day

There aren't many trees or lamposts on the Oakwell pitch, so Toby is well known for cocking his leg on the visitors' goalposts to mark his territory. In 1910 Barnsley had a real donkey mascot – perhaps he was even more messy.

'Who are ya?'
TOBY TYKE

What's in the name?
My dad was a Latin scholar and called me Tobias. The word Tyke can mean various things, including a Yorkshireman and an 'objectionable fellow'. Er, I'm the first of these!

Sponsor
It used to be Winalot but now I have Bryan the Butcher.

What's your trademark?
I run from the halfway line before every match at Oakwell, dispatching the ball into the visitors' goal. I've still to convince a ref that it counts though!

Interests outside football?
Having a few beers with my canine pals on a Friday night and howling all the way home to our kennels.

Love of your life
TINA – what a dresser, what lipstick, what pedigree! Ohhh, where's my water bowl….

Favourite food
Bryan the Butcher's Bangers aren't bad, and I'm quite partial to a bit of next door's cat's bottom when it dares to creep into our garden.

Finest hour
Being chased by a policeman – all I did was throw a bucket of water over him. He got me back though, I'll have his helmet before the season's over!

Highlights of your career…
I turned the Christmas lights on the other year – they were quite high!

Charity and local community work…
Chief fundraiser for the Barnsley Blind Referees' Society

Worst thing about mascot life…
I never seem to moult when the warm weather comes.

Thanks to: Graham Barlow, and Barnsley FC (photos).

Tina keeps Toby on the leash at Oakwell

BIRMINGHAM CITY
BEAU BRUMMIE

'Way to go Brum...'

Beau Brummie once nearly squashed one of Britain's biggest stars as he stumbled when filming with Ant and Dec. Among the 70 other studio guests who did he tumble on? Some singer by the name of Robbie Williams.

'Who are ya?'
BEAU BRUMMIE

What's your trademark?
I'm famous for my run across the pitch before kick off. Visiting teams have come out early just to see it. I can charge about faster than Robbie Savage!

Grand National finishing position?
I stormed home to victory at the first one.

Best mate
Hugh Bear of Warwickshire County Cricket Club – it's good to have a bolt hole in the summer.

Highlights of your career...
The party at the Millennium Stadium when we won promotion to the Prem! I'm also the first mascot to have his portrait painted. Copies will sell in the shops and it really brightens up my kennel!

Worst thing about mascot life...
I came a cropper on my bike at Channel 5's Mascot Knockout, but it was worth it to beat local rival Sky Blue Sam.

Best thing about mascot life...
Getting to kids' parties and shop openings, and putting smiles on people's faces – I like them to be as broad as mine!

Thanks to: Birmingham City FC and Peter Highby.

Guzzle chops – the big mutt celebrates in style after winning the first Mascots' Grand National.

The pride of Lancashire

The spectacular mane of Roar is a link with the red rose of Lancashire, at the heart of the Blackburn club crest. His better half, Roarina, is a lioness who displays the elegance of the rose.

above: The Lion awakes.
Roar welcomes young visitors to Ewood Park

'Who are ya?'
ROAR

Age
I made my debut at Ewood Park in the 1996/97 season and Roarina joined the pride a year later.

What's your trademark?
I have a real lion's roar. Cheltenham's Whaddney was once shown quivering with fear when I demonstrated it on TV.

below: Silky skills from the Lioness. Roarina shows that female mascots can play a bit too.

Interests outside football?
I like sleeping, sleeping and, erm, sleeping!

Love of your life
Football (oops, only kidding Roarina!)

Who do you need to get even with?
Any player who aims a ball at my head.

Highlight of your career...
Roaring the lads to their Worthington Cup victory at the Millennium Stadium!

Worst thing about mascot life...
Getting fur in my mouth. There should be a simpler way of washing!

Best thing about mascot life...
Helping the Derian House Children's Hospice and seeing smiling faces in the crowd.

Thanks to: Blackburn Rovers FC, *Lancashire Evening Telegraph*, Empics.

BLACKPOOL
BLOOMFIELD BEAR

Mascots' merry go round

Blackpool have been through more mascots than managers in recent years. They began with Pip, a huge tangerine, who was replaced with Cable Cat, who then stepped aside for Bloomfield Bear. Bloomfield has made his mark and says he won't be upstaged.

Where's the tuck? Yorkie frisks Bloomfield while Benny Buck and Pilgrim Pete hold him in position.

Officially Bloomfield is a mild-mannered, peanut-butter-loving, cuddly bear, but he's not always a sweet little angel – he once distracted a penalty taker when Tranmere missed a spot kick at Bloomfield Road, and he led the mascots in to dance at Derby's Jubilee celebrations in 2002, when they tried to upstage the cheer leaders at Pride Park. Perhaps it's all part of a misspent youth on Blackpool Pier!

'Who are ya?'
BLOOMFIELD BEAR

Age
I started in 2000 but I'm shy about my actual age – you'll have to check my teeth!

What's your trademark?
My paw print autographs.

Interests outside football?
Acting. I auditioned for Jungle Book 2 but missed out – I had a sore head that day.

Best mate
Tango the Monkey – our junior supporters' mascot.

Highlights of your career
Scoring at the Battle of the Mascots at Shrewsbury in 2000. I raced off in celebration but was soon waddling to a halt as my shorts fell down in front of the packed crowd – some people thought it was rehearsed! I've also recording a single – yes, I broke into voice for that!

In the community...
I'm a patron of the club's local charity 'Donna's Dream House', and I work closely with schools, youth groups and local businesses. Match days can seem like a rest!

Worst thing about mascot life...
Drying out my fur on rainy days.

Thanks to: Helen Wolstencroft, Blackpool FC.

The Lion King

Celebrity Lofty the Lion is much in demand in home-town Bolton. He's a favourite on stage in the Panto, in the classroom with the kids, and on the touchline at the Reebok. He lights up the town wherever he goes.

'Who are ya?'
LOFTY THE LION

What's in the name?

I was named as a tribute to Bolton's club President Nat Lofthouse OBE. Nat was dubbed the Lion of Vienna by the Austrian FA following his part in England's victory over Austria.

What's your trademark?

My body building and my Elvis impersonations. In 2004 I helped promote the new stage production of the Elvis classic Jailhouse Rock.

Highlights of your career...

I've been voted No 1 mascot by the FA and fans, I helped carry the Commonwealth Games baton through Greater Manchester, and I've been voted Bolton's man of the year (well, I'm male, so they said I qualified!).

Civic pride – Lofty and neighbour Fred the Red open Mascot Mania at The Reebok Stadium in 2002, and help to raise over £30,000 for the mayor's charity.

BOLTON WANDERERS
LOFTY THE LION

I've also walked through the Grand Canyon to raise funds for charity, and my band (Lofty the Lion v Pitch Invasion) had a single at no. 54 in the charts.

Best thing about mascot life...
I help raise funds for Coronary Care, Vision Aid, Sargent Trust, CHAT, Child Flight, Christies Hospital, Derian House, Bolton Hospice, and other charities. Also, I help in kicking racism not just out of football, but out of the community.

Word on the street about you...
"If I was running against Lofty for mayor I'd stand no chance!" – *Bolton Councillor John Walshe MBE*

Thanks to: Bolton Wanderers FC, *Bolton Evening News*, Bolton Colour lab and Lofty's minders, Lynn and Charlene.

left: The Lion King – Lofty displays his talents as Elvis. The performance, in 2000, was a highlight on BBC's *Match of the Day* that night.

'Who are ya?'
CHERRY BEAR

Grand National finishing position?
I was 33rd last time I did it. I guess I'm just an average kind of bear!

How will you improve next year?
I'm booked at mascot summer fitness camp. Hope they can put up with my snoring!

In the community...
I've helped out with Children in Need and at other community and charity events. I've also done litter picks and planted bulbs – bears take pride in their territory!

Worst thing about mascot life...
I'm not made for this balmy weather we get on the south coast. If only I could be sheared like a sheep – it's okay for Derby's Rammie!

Best thing about mascot life...
Everyone encourages me to behave like a wild animal!

Thanks to: AFC Bournemouth, Pauline Dighton, Mick Cunningham at Sporting Media, *Bournemouth Daily Echo*.

Mascot blues: Cherry Bear sits in shock after Bournemouth suffer relegation to the third division at Wrexham in April 2002. They bounced back the following season.

BRADFORD CITY
CITY GENT AND BILLY BANTAM

A Magic City Gent

Lenny the City Gent is the mascot world's Hagrid – the kind-hearted bouncer at Hogwarts School of Witchcraft and Wizardry in *Harry Potter*. Lenny does magic and has secret powers too – speech! As a flesh and blood mascot he's able to yell along with the fans at Valley Parade, and with his famous belly, he doesn't need any false padding.

Lenny has other surprises: stashed in his briefcase is an infinite supply of pork pies, as well as lots of tricks learnt from his late father, who was a member of the magic circle. Lenny is a special guy amongst Bradford fans and the mascots.

'Who are ya?'
CITY GENT

What's in the name?

City Gent first appeared as an illustrated character in Bradford City's match-day programmes in the 1960s. A famous club director at the time was a Bradford businessman and sported the hat, briefcase and brolly.

left: Still for a second – a rare moment as Billy and Lenny behave for the cameras.

below: Size matters! Lenny shows why he's good in goal – the belly wobble can put you off your half-time burger as well as your penalty!

When the club introduced mascots in the mid-1990s they asked me to be the real character City Gent – he and I have grown up together ever since!

Nickname

"The Pieman" (and many unprintable things about my waistline!).

Sponsor

Removal company Move it Removal. Their catchphrase is 'If we can move City Gent we can move anybody'!

Grand National finishing position?

I've done all the Grand Nationals but usually come second – well, in the second half. I prefer egg-and-spoon races.

Highlights of your career...

Appearing at most Premiership grounds during Bradford's two seasons in the Premiership. Mind you, it's good to be back with the proper mascots in the Football League (ohh, I should not have said that!). I've done several TV appearances and I was followed by American TV for two days in the build up to the 2003 Grand National.

Who do you need to get even with?

The mascots get on really well together, so don't believe everything you read in the papers.

'Don't answer back!' Lenny deals with the hecklers!

BRADFORD CITY
CITY GENT AND BILLY BANTAM

In the community...
Outside my day job City Gent appears at events like Christmas parties and school fayres, and at local football clubs' trophy nights. I'll soon be running out of tricks!

Best thing about mascot life...
The buzz of a match day or a function when I'm with the supporters and see the happy kids' faces. Good – humoured banter with the visiting fans – that should be what football's all about. A lot of people mistake me for the Bradford & Bingley man, but there's only one City Gent!

'Who are ya?'
BILLY BANTAM

City Gent's best mate is a giant chicken – Billy Bantam. The club's 'Bantams' nickname comes from the link with the colours of a breed of Bantam chickens. Real Bantams were sometimes brought to Bradford City matches by supporters in the 1930s and '40s. Billy Bantam is Lenny's faithful sidekick (sometimes literally). They stir up the crowd together and do a famous belly-bounce wrestle before each match – strangely, Lenny wins every time!

Thanks to: Bradford City FC (photos), Lenny Berry, Lynn Berry, www.kipax.com.

Lenny has his head shaved to raise money for the Club in 2004, while Sheffield Utd's Captain Blade wonders if he's next.

The secrets of the Hive...

TV celeb Graham Norton is not known for his impersonations, although he does dress up quite a bit. However he once did a take-off of BuzzBee – which was quite an honour, as mascots don't shed their skin for anyone! BuzzBee also loaned out his fur for a Bees fan's special moment – he wanted to hide from his girlfriend before making a special request. She was invited onto the pitch to meet BuzzBee, then out popped her man with a wedding proposal. After the stinging surprise it's believed she said 'yes'!

Checking for nectar – BuzzBee inspects the daisies at Griffin Park.

'Who are ya?'
BUZZBEE

What's in the name?
Brentford are the Bees – check out our club crest!

What's your trademark?
My stinger – so don't wind me up!

Interests outside football?
Nectar tasting, and I do a London Parks brand of honey!

Finest hour
Winning a penalty shoot-out at the Millennium Stadium!

Best mate
I've got a soft spot for Harry and Harriet the Hornets of Watford, and for Bertie and Bumble the bees of Burnley, but best of all are the Bees' fans at Griffin Park.

Highlights of your career
Meeting Graham Norton

In the community...
I buzz along to school assemblies, open days, and other events in the area – meeting fellow Bees is the best part of the job.

Thanks to: Brentford FC (photos), Peter Gilham.

BRISTOL CITY
CITY CAT AND CITY KITTY

Cats at the Gate

City Cat and Kitty support their team in front of the Cider Army home and away. Like most moggies, City Cat likes a snooze and has been known to fall asleep on the pitchside at some City games. The shame is that fans have found a giant dozing cat more entertaining than the match!

'Who are ya?'
CITY CAT

What's in the name?
I'm an orphaned alley cat who they let in at Ashton Gate in 1977. I got given the vacant mascot's job and then invited along my lovely feline friend City Kitty.

Grand National finishing position?
43rd from 113 in 2001. Wolfie and me were the only ones who didn't cheat that year!

Finest hour
Breaking up the fight between Wolfie and the Three Little Pigs at Ashton Gate in 1998. Some media reports claimed I'd rushed to join in the fight, but that's not true. I broke it up – I was a national hero!

Who do you need to get even with?
The whole of the Tranmere squad for flattening me at Ashton Gate.

Worst thing about mascot life...
The humiliation often suffered at the hands of players. One example was when Jason McAteer (then of Liverpool) knocked me to the floor in a pre-season friendly. As I picked myself up he then pulled my shorts down!

In the community...
I do as much as I possibly can. I've even helped Bristol Dog's Home!

Word on the street about you...
'Sign him up' – sung by City fans at Blackpool in April 2002. It was half-time and we were losing 4-0!

'You'll never score past me wearing those boots' – the Heybridge Swifts goalkeeper pre-match after mistaking me for a City player in the tunnel prior to our FA Cup match in 2002. Unfortunately for him, Roberts, Murray, Tinnion and Lita were not wearing my boots – we won 7-0!

Thanks to: Bristol City FC.

BOSTON UNTED
PILGRIM PANTHER

The first voyage of English puritans seeking out life in North America was from the small port of Boston in Lincolnshire. These pilgrims soon found themselves clamped in the town's dungeons, and a later voyage of pilgrims from Plymouth to the New World in 1620 (see Pilgrim Pete's part of the book) got more coverage in the history books. The dungeons are near to Boston United's York Street ground, and the club takes its nickname from those Pilgrims.

Late in 2003 a new folk-hero emerged from the dungeons – Pilgrim Panther. He might have been a pirate or a pilgrim, but the fans voted for something different – a Panther! He takes his markings from the black and amber club colours and and in 2004 he teamed up with another modern legend, Gazza!

Thanks to: Boston United FC (photo).

BRISTOL ROVERS
CAPTAIN GAS

Captain Gas is a maritime legend in the port of Bristol – a pirate from the gas works by Bristol Rover's old ground at Eastville. Or is he? He also claims to have started life in 1883 along with the formation of the club itself, who were first known as the Black Arabs. Dubbed 'Gas Head' by the Rovers' fans, the Captain is a friendly rogue. He helps Children in Need and the Kick Racism out of Football campaign. He's also been a deckhand at the port of Bristol on the *Mathew*, although he prefers to command his own ship. He counts beating neighbours Bristol City to clinch promotion as one of his best memories, but he'd be willing to have one of their moggie mascots under his rule as a ship's cat!

Thanks to: Bristol Rovers FC (photo) and Ian Holtby.

BURNLEY
BERTIE BEE AND BUMBLE BEE

Humming on the Turf

The charity Sport Relief once asked Bertie for an interview on TV – he couldn't oblige because he can only buzz, not talk. They wanted to know how he intercepted a streaker at Turf Moor that the stewards couldn't catch. Burnley's Bees are obviously good at homing in on targets.

'Who are ya?'
BERTIE AND BUMBLE

How do you take penalties?
Straight down the middle – bees go direct for their target!

Interests outside football?
Humming tunes, and beating Preston's Deepdale Duck at penalties!

Highlights of your career
Bertie: Tackling a streaker at the Preston NE game in 2001/02.

Bumble: My performances at the Grand National. I'm closing in on a medal position, and my breakdancing and gymnastics are paying off.

Favourite food
Burnley's pies – makes a change from all that rich gooey nectar.

Worst thing about mascot life...
Hibernating in the summer – what a mixed-up life!

Best thing about mascot life...
Performing in front of our fans, appearing at shop openings and doing surprise birthday parties and seeing the joy on children's faces. It gives us a great buzz!

Thanks to: Burnley FC, Empics (hover photo).

Bertie Bee

Bumble Bee

On patrol at Gigg Lane

We've all had our off days, and Robbie's came in 2000 when Cardiff's Bartley the Bluebird (RIP) visited Gigg Lane. The two of them came to blows and the scrap was heard about across Britain, such was the media interest. The incident was certainly out of character and Robbie is now long forgiven. The giant policeman is back on his beat…

'Who are ya?'
ROBBIE THE BOBBY

Thanks to: Martin Ogden (Photos), Bury Times (photo), Gordon Sorfleet, and Bury FC Supporters Trust.

What's in the name?
Sir Robert Peel was born in Bury in 1788. As well as becoming Prime Minister in 1834 he formed the Metropolitan Police Force in 1829. In Victorian times policemen were known as 'Peelers' or, as they still are today, 'Bobbies'. Yep – it came from me!

What's your trademark?
My extremely nice smile – the wind changed direction once and fixed it into place.

How do you take penalties?
I try to deceive the keeper at the last minute. My neighbour Chaddy the Owl has never beaten me!

Grand National finishing position?
I didn't finish because a certain white swan tripped me!

How will you improve next year?
Ambush Cyril before he gets me!

Highlights of your career…
My head was stolen in 2003, and I was shown on telly headless, feeling my way around the streets of Bury in search of it. Plastic surgeons in the area rushed to my help, and fixed me up with a new one just in time for our next match. It doesn't make me look any prettier though.

Best thing about mascot life…
I get to meet all the kids at our games, and I can check that the other police are doing their duty. I also do a lot of work for 'Forever Bury' to promote the club.

The laughing policeman – Robbie on his touchline patrol.

CAMBRIDGE UNITED
MARVIN THE MOOSE

How did a moose from the great outdoors of North America end up at the Abbey Stadium? There's no sign of such a beast on the club crest or in the history of the club. In fact, Marvin emerged from banter on the terraces. It seems that a supporter was at a game, rather smelly, having arrived back from a long spell of travelling, and preferring to watch his team before calling home for a wash. He was told he stank like a moose. It must have been quite a pong, because the term lived on amongst the fans, and they've found plenty of reasons to use it. So out of the derogatory label arrived a mascot, but it hasn't bothered Marvin – with such a background he's nothing to lose!

Thanks to: Cambridge United FC.

A moose in the Fens –
Marvin in party mood at the Abbey Stadium.

CHARLTON ATHLETIC
FLOYD AND HARVEY

Pets on parade

Floyd and Harvey take their names from streets next to Charlton's home at The Valley – Floyd Road and Harvey Gardens. They spend their lives making children happy and helping the Junior Reds. Floyd is the boisterous bulldog, and Harvey the crafty cat.

On match days the two giant pets do warm-ups with the players and enjoy the pre-match photos. Harvey once lined up next to David Beckham, then of Man United, to face the cameras. She trod a clompy mascot boot on his foot – the one with a nagging injury at the time. She claims it was pure accident, and as she supports England, we might just believe her.

The two furballs do hospital visits, attend parties, and even make it to weddings. So, Charlton supporters, beware of gatecrashing bulldogs and alley cats on your special day, and order extra food!

Thanks to: Charlton Athletic FC and Geraldine Clout, Empics (photo).

V(alley) cat –
Harvey waves to the Charlton faithful

CHELSEA
STAMFORD THE LION

Village life

Stamford the Lion is a busy critter meeting the kids at Stamford Bridge on match days.

Stamford is known for his crazy dancing and for his close relationship with the Stamford Ettes. He's led his side out to FA Cup success at Wembley and he enjoys his charity work for the club. Chelsea has a cosmopolitan feel these days with some of the world's top stars amongst the playing staff, but there's no sign yet of a Russian bear teaming up with the English lion.

Thanks to: Mark Taffler, Chelsea FC, Action Images (photo).

Stamford at the Bridge –
Stamford the Lion at his South London pad.

'Who are ya?'
WHADDNEY THE ROBIN

What's in the name?
Cheltenham Town used to be known as the Rubies, but these days our red stripes make us the robins. I'm Whaddney from Whaddon Road – get it?

Love of your life
I'm still looking for something cuddly – and the other football club robins in this part of the world are all male.

Who do you need to get even with?
Exeter's Alex the Greek – when I pinched his trident he grabbed it back, pinned me to the ground, and ran off with my boots. Okay, so he tickled me with his trident but everyone thought he stabbed me – don't tell, because I like the sympathy! There's also a Scunthorpe fan who got me with a direct hit with a pie. It splattered all over my face and only washed off with extra-strong carpet cleaner!

Highlights of your career
I've been to Wembley and the Millennium Stadium, but doing a school pantomime was far more nerve-racking. I'm now hungry for the big stage so am practising dressing up and acting!

Thanks to: Steve Dorrance (cartoon).

THE ADVENTURES OF WHADDNEY

CHESTERFIELD
CHESTER THE FIELD MOUSE

'Who are ya?'
CHESTER
THE FIELDMOUSE

Sponsor
Still looking – I'll take it from anyone as long it's not rodent poison companies!

What's your trademark?
I run up to the crowd and they cheer (sometimes) and I'm also a figure of dancing perfection – all the lady mice swoon when I hit the pitch.

How do you take penalties?
I take penalties like Alan Shearer in his international prime although I have performed the occasional 'Southgate'.

Mighty Mouse – Chester warms up the Gaffer's seat

Interests outside football?
I'm a great fan of Tom and Jerry cartoons – JERRY! JERRY! JERRY!

Who do you need to get even with?
I once squabbled with a certain Tiger but I'm prepared to let it go. More recently, Sammy the Stag beat me in a penalty shoot-out in front of my own fans (see earlier section marked 'Southgate') so it will be nice to get back to the norm of beating him soundly.

Highlights of your career...
Celebrating promotion with the players when we left Division Three: after all the financial worries it was great that the club finally got what it had worked for – I even managed to lose my head I was that excited! Just as pleasing, however, have been my visits to the local children's ward at Chesterfield Royal Hospital. The nurses said that I made the children's day with my antics. Well, they made my year by showing how brave they were in their adversity.

In the community...
I visit schools and youth clubs and other good causes. I also help the Chesterfield Football Supporters' Society who have taken over the running of the club and done such a great job after our recent troubles. They keep me in cheese so I have to be nice to them!

Worst thing about mascot life...
There isn't enough football! Lets not worry about players getting tired – we should be looking at football every day. Except Mondays... Tom and Jerry are on.

Best thing about mascot life...
Definitely the fans – to hear them shout your name and cheer as another penalty bulges the net (see section marked 'Shearer') or to see people smile as I get ticked off for being cheeky is the greatest feeling. Without the fans, Chester, and football, would be nothing.

Word on the street about you...
I was helping Santa Claus arrive in style at a department store in Chesterfield. Afterwards a little lad came up to me and said 'Chester, I like you better than Santa'. It doesn't get any better than that!

Thanks to: Chesterfield FC.

'Who are ya?'
EDDIE THE EAGLE

What's in the name?
The imperial Eagle on the club crest has its origins from the Romans, who founded the town of Colchester.

What's your trademark?
Several other mascots reckon themselves as 'keepers but I'm the best. I save shots like an eagle swooping on its prey.

Interests outside football?
Soaring on the thermals above Layer Road, and catching worms – some managers come to mind!

Finest hour
Bringing down Cambridge's Marvin the Moose at Layer Road. There's several good meals' worth on him!

Best mate
Eddie the Eagle – no not me, the Essex County Cricket one! Watch out when we hunt together!

In the community
I visit schools, give out tickets and help out in everything at Colchester United.

Best thing about mascot life...
I first won round the fans at Layer Road in 1988 when the visiting keeper Scott Howie of Wigan had an injury that took over five minutes to treat. The crowd were getting restless, so even though I was new on the scene I had to do something – I dashed onto the pitch with the stretcher and offered it to the injured player, then I limbered up in the goalmouth as he braced himself for the re-start. The fans roared with approval – phew!

Thanks to: Colchester United FC.

COVENTRY CITY
SKY BLUE SAM

The elephant, castle and St George

Sky Blue Sam is a fitness fanatic and agile dancer – well, he does his best considering he's a lumbering elephant with a mighty appetite. He's also polite and gentle, and has never used his trunk to hose down his opponents, not even in the Grand National to buy himself a few yards. But, there's a first time for everything and no one should risk tugging those ears – an elephant never forgets!

'Who are ya?'
SKY BLUE SAM

After too many craters are found on the pitch, Sam gets lessons as a stadium tour guide.

How do you symbolise your club?
On the city and the club crest is an elephant – a beast so strong that it's carrying a tower – Coventry's castle, full of armed men. The elephant is also on the crest because people believed it could slay dragons. This link with dragon-slaying comes through St George, who slew the dragon and was thought to have been born in Coventry. Hey, perhaps I should be England's patron saint!

How do you take penalties?
With great difficulty – I try not to stamp on the ball but I've burst a few in my time.

Love of your life
Wimbledon's Wandle Womble – she's friendly, cuddly, and used to clearing up mess!

In the community
I visit schools to encourage healthy eating, I've switched on the Christmas lights and I take part in the Coventry Fun Run.

Worst thing about mascot life...
When Coventry lose – I wish an elephant did forget sometimes!

Best thing about mascot life...
Showing off my belly bounce!

Thanks to: Coventry City FC (photo).

CRYSTAL PALACE
PETE THE EAGLE AND ALICE THE EAGLE

Eagle territory

Pete is an old stager who began at Selhurst Park in the early 1980s. He's had a couple of facelifts since, and his ladyfriend Alice teamed up with him in 2001. With the club back in the top flight for 2004/05 the eagles are soaring at Palace.

Pete is a celeb in his own right – his photograph has been all over the London Underground promoting a new habitat for water birds in south-west London. He's also starred in a TV advert for coke – but just how he got a craving for the brown fizzy stuff isn't clear.

Alice from the Palace now sports a wedding ring on her claws, and she and Pete are having a mascot wedding like no other. Watch out for a real mascot hen night and stag night – sounds wild!

Thanks to: Crystal Palace FC.

CREWE ALEXANDRA
GRESTY THE LION

DARLINGTON
MR Q

Laughing Lion

Gresty is Crewe's lively lion from Gresty Road. He's been one of the leading comic acts amongst the mascots and still finds time to help local charities and good causes. He came 6th in his Grand National appearance, even with a sprained ankle, and his highlight was the 1997 Wembley play-off promotion to the First Division when he was just a lion cub. He rates Wolves' Wolfie as his best pal, even though he says he's got scars on his fur from when Mr Wolf pounced on him.

Thanks to: Crewe Alexandra FC, *Crewe Chronicle*.

Hats off to the Quakers

The Victorian industrialists of Darlington included many Quakers – a branch of the Christian faith which has no written creed and no ministers. The world's first railway was laid from Darlington in 1825, and this helped generate much of the industry in the town. The club's Feethams ground was acquired from a prominent industrialist and Quaker, John Pease, and the club marks those connections with its nickname of 'the Quakers'. Today at the Feethams, Mr Q the Quaker keeps the link with John Pease alive. Only one mascot's hat rivals the traditional tall Quaker hat of Mr Q – check out Plymouth's Pilgrim Pete.

Thanks to: Darlington FC, Richard Parkes.

Citizen Ram

The four-legged Derby Ram is a military hero and a hard act to follow. The two-legged Rammie is out on the streets and in the dales of Derbyshire, helping charities and taking reading classes in schools. Rammie is the people's mascot and a football hero – he'll get his medals too!

'Who are ya?'
RAMMIE

What's your trademark
The sportsmanship I show towards the away supporters – I always invite five children from the away crowd to take part in a penalty shootout. Everyone scores and gets a certificate.

Highlights of your career...
Being voted the most popular Premiership mascot amongst supporters when Derby were in the top flight. Winning the Pudsey Stakes race at Nottingham race track against Sherwood the Bear of Nottingham Forest and Mr and Mrs Magpie of Notts County. Presenting Robert Lindsey with a signed Derby County shirt at the Palladium when he played Fagin in Oliver. Leading my team through the streets of Derby in 1995/96 season when we were promoted to the Premiership. Making my first children's video/DVD with positive learning messages throughout.

In the community...
I help with all local charities and provide match tickets, footballs and shirts. I run a 'Reading is Fun' campaign in over 200 schools across four counties. It helps motivate kids and show them what fun reading can be. I also take school assemblies encouraging children to cross the road properly and not to talk to strangers. I help to host around 200 parties at Pride Park each year, for young and old, and I attend weddings, christenings and even 100th birthdays!

Best thing about mascot life...
Making a difference to people's lives. Yes, mascots really can do that!

PRIVATE DERBY THE RAM

Private Derby is the regimental mascot of the Worcestershire & Sherwood Foresters, the County Regiment of Derbyshire. In 1858, the 95th Derbyshire Regiment was operating in Central India, during the Indian Mutiny campaign. The Commanding Officer noticed a fine fighting ram tethered in a yard. He directed Private Sullivan to take the ram, and it followed him quite contentedly, marching nearly 3,000 miles. It was present with the 95th Regiment in six actions and in 1862 it received, with the rest of the battalion, the Indian Medal.

Read along with Rammie – one of the giant Ram's popular reading sessions.

DERBY COUNTY
RAMMIE

The first Private Derby fought 33 battles with other rams and was never defeated. But alas, he was accidentally drowned by jumping over a wall into a well at Hyderabad in 1863.

Since 1912 the Duke of Devonshire has presented each new Private Derby ram from his Swaledale flock at the Chatsworth estate. Private Derby rarely visits the team on match days as they seem to lose each time he comes.

Thanks to: Derby County FC, Dean Mottram, *Derby Evening Telegraph*, Major J.O.M. Hackett.

Four legs and shaggy! The 27th of the Private Derby rams – a famous part of Derby County's club crest.

Dodgy keeper? Everyone gets a certificate for scoring past Rammie.

bottom: Ram with a mission – Rammie promotes food collection for Derby City Mission.

DONCASTER ROVERS
DONNY DOG

GILLINGHAM
TOMMY T TREWBLU

Thanks to: Empics (photo).

Tommy cantered into the Priestfield Stadium in 1999, but he represents a much older horse, dating from 1066, when William the Conqueror was crowned King of England. At that time the county of Kent was left unconquered by William and his Norman invaders, as symbolised by the white Invicta (untamed horse) on the crest of Kent and the Gillingham club badge.

Tommy meets the Gills' young fans on match days and at soccer schools. He's been to two Wembley play-off finals and appeared in Ant and Dec's Slap Bang mascot special. Tommy is becoming slightly tamer these days, but Kent remains unconquered!

Thanks to: Gillingham FC.

below right: Neigh money – Tommy outside Carlton's offices in 2002, helping the Football League draw attention to the effects of the collapsed financial deal with ITV Digital.

below: Donny bounds onto the Belle Vue turf.

GRIMSBY TOWN
MIGHTY MARINER

Mighty is a cross between Captain Birds Eye and a sailor-mariner. He's also been likened to Uncle Albert on TV comedy show *Only Fools and Horses*. But Mighty is not a grumpy old geezer who just sits in the corner. He's a timeless lucky charm at Blundell Park.

'Who are ya?'
MIGHTY MARINER

What's in the name?
Our nickname is the Mariners because of Grimsby's great tradition as a fishing port, and we have a trawler on our club crest.

What's your trademark?
Pole-dancing around the goalpost! No, it's not an ancient ritual here at Blundell Park but something that shows my vigour, despite the whiskers and wrinkles!

How do you take penalties?
I blast them – and I'm used to mending nets!

Grand National finishing position?
About halfway – impressive for a pensioner!

Favourite food
It's got to be our local delicacy here in Cleethorpes: fishcakes!

In the community...
I visit local schools and factories, and I'll go anywhere to meet a Grimsby Town fan.

I won a prize for most money raised for charity in the 2002 Mascots' Grand National, all in aid of a local children's hospice.

Thanks to: Jonathan Moscrop, Grimsby Town FC.

The bearded wonder –
are they pom poms, or bits of Mighty's beard?

Two monkeys, one tale...

The tale of H'Angus is incredible – the origin of the monkey way back in 1800 is special enough, but in 2002 as the people of Hartlepool voted for their mayor, the events were sensational...

In the early nineteenth century British ships fought to stop Napoleon and his French forces invading England. At that time a monkey got washed ashore from a shipwreck off the Hartlepool coast. The local fisherman had never seen such a creature and thought he was a Frenchman in disguise, sent by Bonaparte to spy on them. They took no chances and hanged the poor creature on the beach. People from Hartlepool have been referred to as 'monkey hangers' ever since, and the football club honoured the legendary monkey in their mascot, H'Angus.

H'Angus arrives
The monkey mascot came to Hartlepool's Victoria Park in 1999. H'Angus helped pump up the crowd on match days and quickly became everyone's friend.

H'Angus was also busy in the community, helping raise funds for good causes at the club and in the town. He bravely abseiled down Hartlepool's Hillcarter Hotel, and did a gruelling sponsored walk to the club's away match at York, where he was met by best friend Yorkie the Lion.

But he was a cheeky monkey too. His lively behaviour sometimes got him into bother, and he was ejected from two grounds – Blackpool and Scunthorpe – for his high spirits. He enjoyed friendly sparring with opposition mascots, and his reputation as a wild as well as a playful critter grew. He even became a well-known caller to Radio 5's post-match phone-in 606, hosted at the time by Stuart Littlejohn and David Mellor.

It was clear that H'Angus was a creature of spirit and adventure. But in what followed we were to find out just how bold the great ape had become.

Vote H'Angus – was he serious? Could he win?

In 1999, London's Ken Livingstone was the first in a new system of directly elected mayors. In 2002, eleven more towns introduced elections for mayor, including Hartlepool. H'Angus's wearer Stuart Drummond had already considered standing as a monkey candidate at the previous general election, but realised the chances of toppling the town's MP Peter Mandelson were very slim, given his high profile in the Labour Party. But an election for the town's mayor was different – this gave Stuart, and H'Angus, a sporting chance.

A ship's mascot monkey is the only survivor from a shipwreck off Hartlepool in 1803 – the brave little critter met with a tragic end but the legend of H'Angus was born.

HARTLEPOOL UNITED
H'ANGUS THE MONKEY

So what had been an idea and a joke in the pub was put to the test – Stuart Drummond campaigned as H'Angus, and Hartlepool United put up the £500 deposit for their cult mascot to front Stuart's campaign.

Stuart's electioneering was serious, but not as active as other local candidates. United kept their distance from the campaign, letting Stuart and H'Angus do their own thing. The club stressed they were simply hosting a fringe candidate and not trying to ridicule local politics.

As the election campaign developed, the interest in H'Angus swelled. Local bookmakers had refused to take odds on the monkey candidate, but a web-based bookie offered 100/1 on a H'Angus victory. Knowing that Stuart might be in with a shout, people rushed to take advantage of these odds. Reacting fast, the bookmaker slashed the price, before suspending bets. The local paper seized upon this story, and word got about: H'Angus had a chance!

Jungle fever

Running up to the 2 May election the heat was on. In his day job, twenty-eight-year-old Stuart was a credit controller in a call centre; now he was having to face questions central to the future of the town. Meanwhile the national media were clamouring for his attention, and into the bargain H'Angus was needed for the club's crucial promotion play-off campaign. On one night Stuart missed a vital debate with other candidates so H'Angus could be at the club's play-off game in Cheltenham.

But the mascot man was coping well – support from the town's football fraternity remained solid, and Stuart's common sense and conviction were winning people round. The prospect of victory didn't seem so daft.

The night of the election was high drama – H'Angus beat off the Labour challenge by 7,395 to 6,792 votes and an astonished Hartlepool woke up to their monkey mayor. Papers reported the bizarre events under

Tug o' tail – best mates H'Angus and Yorkie argue over who's king of the jungle.

headlines of 'Banana Drama', 'Monkey Business', 'Yes, we have no bananas', 'Apeing politicians', and 'Banana Republic'. But was it now time for the victorious Stuart Drummond to shed his monkey skin and take the mayor's role as his own?

That morning the nation's media descended on Hartlepool to get the story. Most papers were desperate for the monkey and his pledge of free bananas to live on. A week of intense media scrutiny followed, as reporters across the world learnt of the spectacular events in Hartlepool. Again the questions came – was it the monkey or the man inside who would be mayor? But Stuart knew the rules had changed: he had a new challenge, and H'Angus, such a part of his personality over the past three years, would remain at the club – there was no transfer for H'Angus to the Town Hall. Stuart was determined to respect the mayoral position and do the best for his town.

The price of politics

Stuart Drummond's electioneering campaign cost nothing – probably a first in politics, and a testament to the monkey that he made come to life. £100 was raised through sales of H'Angus election rosettes, and the club donated this and the £500 returned deposit to Stuart's number one cause – the club's Disabled Supporters' Association.

Two years into the job the young mayor had not been fazed by his duties and the pressures of managing the Council's £100m budget. His work has involved improving sports facilities for the town's young people, testing a compulsory landlord registration scheme and getting young offenders doing graffiti clear-up. His primate past is not forgotten, and his passion for the club remains, but his status as a political leader is what's developing now.

Monkey Manifesto – H'Angus sets out his politically delicious offer to the Hartlepool electorate.

Just the ticket – H'Angus and club shop manageress Sharon Precious present Anthony Keir with a season ticket donated by a fan.

H'Angus for Mayor
YOUR VOTE COUNTS

I pledge to reduce the number of councillors on the Council.

Better sports facilities and more activities for the town's youngsters

I promise free bananas for all schoolchildren during their break.

People have said for years that a monkey could be elected in Hartlepool now we're going to find out.

Stuart Drummond will stand under his own name but campaign as H'Angus using the slogan:

"Vote for H'Angus He gives a monkey's."

Follow his campaign at : www.hartlepoolunited.co.uk

HARTLEPOOL UNITED
H'ANGUS THE MONKEY

A new plot and a new cast...

Meanwhile, H'Angus the Monkey needed recasting at Hartlepool. The club grabbed more headlines when they let candidates audition for the role of the ape in pre-season friendlies. H'Angus then returned to looking after his club and helping in the community. He also got an invite as mystery guest on BBC TV's *They Think it's All Over*, being stroked and petted by blinfolded celebs in front of millions! The club then had a triumphant season in 2002/03, easing to promotion from Division Three. The great ape was already heading for new adventures.

Election fever –
Hartlepool fans spread the word about their primate hero

Special thanks to Stuart Drummond, Paul Mullen, Gordon Robinson, North News, *Hartlepool Mail*, David Carless, Frank Reid.

left: Banana bombshell! The local paper declares the incredible result, and the rest is history.

On the scent of victory – H'Angus recruits Freddy Fox of Halifax as his election agent!

HUDDERSFIELD TOWN
TERRY AND TRISHA

Yorkshire Grit

Huddersfield branded themselves The Terriers in 1969. They re-introduced the blue and white stripes and added a terrier to the club crest. A supporter's dog, Skippy, became the first Terrier mascot and was used as the model for the crest. Skippy was described at the time as 'an appealing dog with all the grit and determination in the world'. Terry and Trisha carry on the tradition and provide the grit today.

'Who are ya?'
TERRY AND TRISHA THE TERRIERS

What's in the name?
We've taken over from Skippy – he was a pedigree Yorkshire Terrier and a hard act to follow.

What's your trademark?
Terry: A run and slide after a goal.
Trisha: A yap and howl after a goal.

Interests outside football?
Terry: Rolling in mud.
Trisha: Lounging in the grooming parlour.

Favourite food
Linesman's ankles.

Who do you need to get even with?
Terry: The Bristol City sub who knocked my head off in a warm up!
Trisha: Anyone who's rude about my hair!

Best thing about mascot life...
All the fuss and attention, and getting our tummies tickled! Terriers are sociable dogs so we like to help at community events.

Thanks to: Huddersfield Town FC, *Huddersfield Examiner*.

Mutts at the McAlpine – Terry and Trisha after obedience class.

HUDDERSFIELD TOWN
TERRY AND TRISHA

True Terrier – The four legged Skippy with his owner Beryl Fisher at a presentation to club captain Jimmy Nicholson in 1970. Photos of Skippy were used to design the Terrier on the club crest.

Tricia shows off her new hair-do at the Millenium Stadium, where Huddersfield clinched promotion in 2004.

HULL CITY
ROARY THE TIGER

He's Grrrrreat!

There's a famous tiger who does telly adverts and peers at us from breakfast cereal packs. Hull's Roary is not to be upstaged by this rival though – Roary's not a cartoon, he's for real!

'Who are ya?'
ROARY THE TIGER

What's in the name?
The *Hull Daily Mail* newspaper once started to call Hull City the tigers because of their amber and black colours. The name stuck, and in 1998 I turned up to roar them on.

Finest hour
Leading Hull City out for their first game at the new Kingston Communications Stadium in front of 22,000 fans!

Who do you need to get even with?
Lincoln's Poacher the Imp – he beat me at penalties. I wouldn't have minded much but it was on telly!

Highlights of your career...
I got to shake paws with Hull's past players at 'the walk of legends' at the club's last game at Boothferry Park.

Getting ambushed by players when I was once doing my washing, and seeing them have a go at being Roary!

Inviting a young lad to give me a pretend punch, and knocking myself out when I fell to the floor.

Best thing about mascot life...
Travelling to away games and greeting those special fans who follow the team everywhere. I help out local causes as much as I can, and I've done a sponsored abseil – all part of the grrrrreat job.

Thanks to: Hull City FC.

Amber alert – Roary leads out his team at the KC Stadium.

Noble steeds

Bluey and Crazee come from the Suffolk Punch horse on the Ipswich crest. The strong Suffolk Punch breed of horses were popular with the heavily armoured knights of medieval England. King Richard I bred Suffolks and they were the most popular sporting horses till the reign of Henry VIII – and they even managed to carry his eighteen-stone weight. Bluey and Crazee keep the fine reputation of the breed going at Portman Road.

Thanks to: Iah Dawson, Lime Technologies, Ipswich Town FC (photos).

'Who are ya?'
BLUEY AND CRAZEE HORSE

Shadey Character – Crazee Horse

Age
We're ancient breeds, but forever young!

How do you take penalties?
We hoof them in while the goalkeeper isn't looking!

Grand National finishing position?
Don't mention the Grand National – there's extra pressure on us actual horses to win it.

How will you improve next year?
Learn to handle the pressure, be better shod, or maybe just enter a proper horse race!

Favourite food
We get fed lots of chocolate by supporters – makes a change from all the hay!

Highlights of your career...
Bluey made the victorious Wembley play-off final in 2000, and together with hundreds of children he welcomed the Queen's helicopter on her Golden Jubilee visit to Ipswich. In 2004 we starred in a TV documentary and showed what it's like to be mascot stars.

Worst thing about mascot life...
Mucking out the stable.

Best thing about mascot life...
Meeting young supporters and members of the Blues Crew. We help in the community with anything from village fêtes, carnivals, birthday parties, hospital visits and lots more.

KIDDERMINSTER HARRIERS
HARRY THE HARRIER

Mighty Harry

Harry swooped down to Aggborough in 1997. He's a whopping 7 feet tall and sixteen stone, and his poor eyesight is a big disadvantage for a hawk needing to swoop on its prey. He may have a hard exterior but he can be sensitive too – you'll see he's been moved to poetry later in the book.

'Who are ya?'
HARRY THE HARRIER

What's in the name?
Harrier comes from the club's roots as an athletics club called the Harriers and Harry just seemed to fit.

What's your trademark?
I'm renowned for showing a 'cheeky' area of my body to the away fans!

Grand National finishing position?
In the 2001 race I was in the thick of the early pile-up, but dragged myself up and finished. I improved in 2002, but I'm big and heavy, so if you consider my extreme weight disadvantage I'm easily worth a top-three finish!

Highlights of your career
Some of the opposition are fooled into thinking I'm a softie but they soon come unstuck... can you remember coming out to play at Aggborough little Cheltenham Robin? Never try and shoulderbarge the big bird because you'll only get into a flap!

Who do you need to get even with?
I once had a little scrape with Swansea's Cyril after penalties. I might have lost my head but Cyril took a bump when I came crashing down on top of him. Anyway, Harry 2 goals, Cyril 1.

Best thing about mascot life...
Running onto the sacred turf, mingling with the players, having fun with the crowd, acting as daft as I like and being proud to wear the colours of my club! I'm also a community-minded sole and help out in charity events and school fêtes.

Thanks to: Kidderminster Harriers FC, and the *Kidderminster Shuttle/Times and News*.

Backseat driver – Harry reckons his Harry Mobile is classier than the players' motors.

The nutty fox

They may be nicknamed the Foxes, but Leicester were once 'the nutters', with the filbert and other types of nut appearing on street names around the famous old Filbert Street stadium. The fox is now the symbol of the club, and including a 1940s fox mascot, Leicester have now had four of the creatures patrolling the touchline.

The Quorn is one of the oldest fox hunts in the country, and has made its mark on the fox symbols of Leicestershire and Leicester City. Filbert is fox number one at the club, busy supporting Leicester City's work in the community from his smart new den at Filbert Way. He's a well-loved figure in the county, doing school visits, reading lessons, and teaming up with Leicester legend Alan Birchenall to welcome fans on match days – the Quorn Hunt will not be chasing him!

Lapping it up – Filbert and girlfriend Vicky Vixen celebrate the second of Leicester City's Worthington Cup prizes in Martin O'Neil's era.

LEYTON ORIENT
THEO THE WYVERN

What's a Wyvern?

A wyvern is a mythical creature, half dragon and half serpent. In Orient's case, the dragon represents the crest of the City of London, whilst the serpent represents Orient's connections with the sea – the Orient Shipping Company and P&O Group, from which the club takes its name. Out of all this comes Theo, a mighty wyvern: now you know the difference, don't risk calling him a dragon!

'Who are ya?'
THEO

What's in the name?
The club's nickname is 'The O's'.

Age
I've been prowling around the kingdom of London for centuries and settled in my cave at Leyton Orient in 1998.

Interests outside football
Keeping my cave beneath the pitch tidy in the hope it will attract a Mrs Theo! I'm insisting the cave is rebuilt when the ground is re-developed. It's environmentally friendly so I don't expect problems with the planners.

Finest Hour
Breaking up a fight at a match against local rivals Southend. I'm a good friend of the police and stewards now, even if I do torment linesmen!

Highlights of your career
Drenching the O's public address announcer before a game, and breaking his clipboard in front of all the fans. He tries to get me back but I'm too smart! Capturing Athena the Goddess of Exeter, but don't mention it to Alex her bodyguard – the pictures show he slayed me but I'm a good actor, and I got Athena's number!

Best thing about mascot life
Being able to smile all day long no matter how you feel, and joining in as many young fans' parties as I can.

Thanks to: Leyton Orient FC, Daniel Roper, and Matt Porter.

Theo leads the line at Sport relief's 2004 London mile run.

Grotesquely funny

From deepest Lincolnshire comes the mysterious Poacher the Imp. Angels at Lincoln Cathedral once froze a naughty imp, leaving him in stone for centuries. So Poacher makes up for his trapped friend with his wild behaviour. He's also got a crazy dance to the tune of 'The Lincolnshire Poacher', which involves mixing old-style morris dancing with east-coast, gangster-rap style boogie. Poacher is very, very ugly, but, like the film star Shrek, the equally hideous green ogre, someone just might take a liking to him one day. Meanwhile, don't upset the angels…

'Who are ya?'
POACHER THE IMP

What's in the name?
Poacher comes from an old song, 'The Lincolnshire Poacher', which tells the story of a poacher living in Lincolnshire in the nineteenth century. The imp is a character carved in stone at the Angel Chapel in our beautiful cathedral.

What's your trademark?
I'm just over six foot high, but my girth is something to marvel at! I can't actually fit through a standard-size door opening.

How do you take penalties?
I can't see the ball or the goal when I take a penalty, so it's often hit-and-miss. I try to save penalties from our matchday mascots, but even four-year-olds rattle them past me. Mind you, my stunning penalty in 2002/03 against Hull's Roary the Tiger featured on ITV's Goals on Sunday programme, so it's not all bad!

Highlights of your career…
Filming for the FA Cup programmes with other mascots at Wembley in 2000. There I was, holding the FA Cup in the royal box representing the mighty Imps! None of our boys have ever been to Wembley, and it was the old dame's last FA Cup year. My mate tried to take a picture and jammed the lens cap. I still don't speak to him these days – very bitter. Once in a match against Millwall I was escorted off the pitchside by a police officer – the linesman had called me offside twice in the first ten minutes! I love doing school fêtes, kids' parties, and charity football games: I've got to show my pretty face around the neighbourhood!

Thanks to: Chris Vaughan (photos), Alan Long, Rob Bradley, Graham and Andrew Vaughan, and Andy Townsend. Thanks also to the board, chairman and supporters – Poacher says you're the best!

What, no carvings? Poacher checks the Millenium stadium roof for stone imps.

LUTON TOWN
HAPPY HARRY

'Who are ya?'
HAPPY HARRY

What's with the hat?
Luton was once home to a flourishing hat-making industry and we're known as the Hatters – I wear a big straw boater to prove it.

Grand National finishing position?
14th – and my hat stayed on!

How will you improve next year?
Spend less time chatting up the girls from The Sun before the race. Actually, on second thoughts…

Cheeky chappy – Harry warms up at Kenilworth Road.

Interests outside football?
I DJ in a couple of local bars and run an under-8s football team – not easy when you're mute!

Finest hour
When I learnt I was to represent England in the Shotokan Euro championships.

Who do you need to get even with?
Kevin Nicholls at the club – he took my head off live on TV – very painful! The fans loved seeing me running about like a headless chicken though!

Highlights of your career…
Beating Jude the Cat in a penalty shoot out in front of 2000 Luton fans at QPR's Loftus Road. The fans went wild so I had to improve my celebration technique!

Worst thing about mascot life…
Getting my hat nicked. Don't people know it's a vintage model?

Best thing about mascot life…
The buzz from having my name chanted by the fans, and helping with school and community events.

Thanks to: Luton Town FC, Empics (main photo).

'Who are ya?'
ROARY THE LION

What's in the name?
It's because lions roar – well I do anyway! And I'm the lion off the club's crest.

What's your trademark?
Schoolboy errors, blowing my nose on corner flags, and warming up with substitutes.

Roary celebrates finishing at the 2003 Mascots on Wheels race.

Grand National finishing position?
I haven't run the National because I couldn't ever get transport. But now that I've got my lion's driving licence, God help the rest of the competitors!

Best mate
Lenny the Lion from Shrewsbury Town and that Tiger from Hull... what's his name? Oh yeah – Roary!

Favourite food
KitKats, chicken balti pies, and the children who pull my tail.

Who do you need to get even with?
The number 5 from Rochdale because he slapped me. Very unwise!

Highlights of your career...
Winning the Supporters' Club 2002/03 special award, turning on the Christmas lights in Macclesfield, and getting interviewed by ITV digital for the *Football First* programme.

Lion's logic – Skipper Martin Carruthers takes advice from Roary before kick-off.

Worst thing about mascot life...
The 'clever' kids who think I'm not real. And by far the most frustrating thing is that they don't sell bags big enough for me to travel in!

Best thing about mascot life...
The freedom, playing jokes, the things I can get away with, making people laugh, and helping schools and shops in the community. It's a great life.

Thanks from Roary to: Matt Lenton, Thomas Rance, Mum, Roary's great fans, the brilliant kids, and all at Macclesfield Town Football Club.

MANCHESTER CITY
MOONCHESTER AND MOONBEAM

From a galaxy far far away.....

Moonchester and Moonbeam are the only mascots to come from another world. They are weird aliens with awesome powers, who've taken to life in Manchester, where they like the spicy food, the night life and sometimes even the football.

'Who are ya?'
MOONCHESTER

What's in the name?
Our club's anthem is Blue Moon, so I'm an alien from the Blue Moon. So it's a cross between the Moon and Manchester... geddit?

Heavenly bodies –
Moonchester shows he knows who's boss

What's your trademark?
I wiggle my head from side to side, which is strange but keeps the fans happy so I ain't gonna stop!

How do you take penalties?
I just smack'em with the power of Anelka and the skill of Shaun Goater... I sometimes score, so at least it works.

Grand National finishing position?
I came 55th last time I did it. However, this was because I didn't cheat, unlike another Manchester mascot who ran AROUND the hurdles. I can't name names... Oh well, Fred the Red from Manchester United, the red one with the tail, from Manchester United. That's U-N-I-T-E-D.

Love of your life
There are so many I don't know where to start... Ouch! After being given a big dig in the arm I've been forced to say Moonbeam!

Who do you need to get even with?
Fred the Red:
First, he cheated in the Mascot Grand National
Second, he's from Man United
Third, he supports Man United
Fourth, he's cheated
Fifth, I don't need any more reasons!

In the community...
I take part in lots of charity events – one of the highlights is 'When You Wish Upon a Star' when we take terminally ill children to Manchester Airport for their visit to Lapland.

Highlights of your career
Seeing Moonchester tattoos on middle-aged men's arms! At Burnley I was right next to the goal when City's Shaun Goater scored a cracker – he ran straight over and celebrated with me live on TV! It was good for his image to be seen with a star like Moonchester, of course! I carried the Commonwealth Games baton past Maine Road on the morning the games opened in Manchester. I had a few pictures taken with Shaun Goater and the captain of the ladies footy team. I then carried the baton through the streets of Moss Side. Even though it was 6am, everyone had come out their houses to cheer me on. I was over the moon (pardon

the pun). However, had I known David Beckham was carrying it later I would have run the other way! Manchester held an MCFC *v.* MUFC legends match in aid of the New York firefighters. I was standing backstage meeting the guests and VIPs and as usual I decided to ruffle some bloke's hair and noticed a lot of people looking very nervous. Little did I realise I had picked on the US Ambassador, and the 'blokes' around him were actually from the Secret Service!

Word on the street about you...
'You are the best. You ARE the best.' – *David Bernstein*, former chairman MCFC

'Sorry Moonie, you can't get a game today – I know I know, maybe another time.' – *Kevin Keegan*, manager, hero and god.

'Who are ya?'
MOONBEAM

What's your trademark?
Big ears and a big blue bow – there's a cool dress sense on the Blue Moon!

How do you take penalties?
Badly – so I mostly leave it to Moonie, who's not quite as bad. I'm a more highly-evolved alien and am superior to Moonie in all other respects though, including saving penalties!

Highlights of your career
Beating Fred the Red in the mascot race at the Commonwealth Games Trials – and he won't be able to get revenge – hee hee! Running round the pitch with the City team and the Division One Trophy in April 2002

Word on the street about you...
'See you've got your woman with you Moonie – hope you're looking after her!' – *Kevin Keegan*

Thanks to: Manchester City FC, Ed Garvey and Richard Parkes (photos).

Leaving home – Moonchester helps the farewell party at Maine Road go with a bang.

MANCHESTER UNITED
FRED THE RED

Talk of the Devil

Could anyone possibly be more popular than the players and more respected than Sir Alex Ferguson at Manchester United? Yeah, Fred the Red of course! Fred started life in 1994 but there were mascots at United as early as 1902, with a St Bernard dog, 'The Major', followed by a goat, Billy. They had four legs, but Fred is slightly better at penalties.

'Who are ya?'
FRED THE RED

What's in the name?
In the late 1960s Manchester United changed their nickname from the Babes to the Red Devils. The club badge was re-designed in 1970 and included a red devil in the centre. I'm that devil with a furry pitchfork!

What's your trademark?
I do a mascot moonwalk – the best on the planet!

How do you take penalties?
With the arrogance of Cantona and the confidence of Van Nistelrooy!

Fred's day job – the stadium may be quiet but Fred's hard at work for a good cause.

Grand National finishing position?
46th in 2002 – ahead of Manchester City's Moonchester, who did his best to beat me – which, as usual, was just not good enough! In 2003 I beat him too – okay, so he couldn't make it, but I'll count that one as well.

Interests outside football?
I do lots of different events, from shop openings to children's parties, and even weddings at Old Trafford!

Highlights of your career
The treble: I'll never forget that night in Barcelona in 1999 when we snatched victory in stoppage time against Bayern Munich – our boys did us proud! Facing penalties against Coronation Street stars Kevin Webster, Martin Platt and Tyrone Dobbs was great in 2003 at Ryan Giggs' testimonial. They're all United fans but they showed me no mercy!

Word on the street about you...
'The lad shows real potential. He'll be at Manchester United for a long time.' – *Sir Alex Ferguson*

Diary of a Devil
Below are extracts from a year in the life of Fred. We picked 2002 as a typically exciting year…

Jan 2002 – Victory is sweet
At the start of 2002 I was asked by The Disney Channel to appear in their *Mascot Cup* show, featuring mascots from across the country in a penalty shoot-out. I beat Rangers' Broxi Bear and won the Mascot Cup – Yesssss! (were you watching, Moonchester and Chaddy?). Disney asked me back for their *Kids Awards 2002* – I met lots of celebrities, including Gareth Gates and the S Club Juniors!

November 2002 – Kidz Up North
In November I went to Bolton's Reebok Stadium with Football in the Community for 'Kidz Up North'. It's the only UK event totally dedicated to the needs of children with disabilities. I spent the day meeting the children and playing footy with them.

Children in Need
Also in November I took part in the Children in Need Challenge at Man City's Maine Road. We raised lots of money and in the evening I hosted a Children in Need disco at Old Trafford, along with Pudsey Bear himself.

December 2002 – Christmas songs
In December UEFA filmed a *Fred the Red Christmas special*, in which you got to see my office which overlooks the pitch. We also visited Alf Kauffman School in Rochdale, for children with disabilities, which was about to close down. The children and teachers sang Christmas songs and gave us an unforgettable day!

Santa's helper
During the festive season I turned on the Christmas lights in many local towns, attended Christmas fayres, and helped Santa give out pressies in his grotto at the Museum. He's funny, red and famous like me.

MANCHESTER UNITED
FRED THE RED

March 2003 – Pancake Parade
Comic Relief is always a busy date in my calendar –
I took part in a Mascot Pancake Race on Shrove
Tuesday, with a certain big-eared blue mascot taking
the trophy. Then, on St Patricks Day, I went to Ireland to
take part in a Comic Relief Parade.

Throughout the year...
UNICEF is Manchester United's official charity, so I do
as much as I can to help with the fundraising. Apart
from this, I like to help out in every charity event I can. I
visit local schools and colleges through United's Football
in the Community scheme. It's one of the highlights of
my job as I meet the fans face-to-face and I get to
improve my furry soccer skills.

You can write to Fred at: Fred The Red, Manchester
United, Sir Matt Busby Way, Old Trafford, Manchester,
M16 0RA.

Thanks to: Manchester United FC (photos), Kellogg's (Sprint photo).

right: Dare devil – Fred abseils down Old Trafford's South Stand to raise money for Marie Curie Cancer Care.

below: Mascots on their marks – Fred lines up with his North-West rivals at the Kellogg's Mascot Sprint at Lancashire CCC in August 2003. Chaddy the Owl took the honours in a warm up for the Grand National.

MIDDLESBROUGH
ROARY THE LION

Down by the Riverside

Mascots don't come any greater and wiser than Middlesbrough's Roary. He takes reading in schools, works with the local police and has his own programme on telly. He's a hero on Teeside, the kids adore him, and they chose his name in a local paper's competition when he began life in 1995. But there's one section of the community who are not so keen to see him – teachers. They get shown up on a popular part of his TV show when kids get their own back in 'Beat the Teacher'. Don't miss it!

'Who are ya?'
ROARY

How do you symbolise your club?
I bring the lion on the club badge to life at The Riverside. Actually, the creature on the town and club crest might be a Griffin, but we don't look too hard as it's a bit late for me to change form.

Interests outside football?
Although I'm a very quiet lion I encourage children to read. They motivate me to be a good mascot so I like paying them back with some help. I do sign language and I have a brilliant time with my friends with hearing difficulties.

Lion helps bear – Roary helps Pudsey's big brother raise funds for Children in Need.

Finest hour

Going to Wembley three times in one year and proving our fans are the best!

Best mates

The local police force mascot PC Billy Bear and his pal Badgie. We do citizenship days together, like explaining to children that they shouldn't drop litter.

Who do you need to get even with?

Our goalkeeping coach Paul Barron. He aims for my head in warm-ups and thinks it's good luck if he hits it!

Highlights of your career...

I was the first mascot to walk through the Houses of Parliament and I had tea on the terraces there with Stuart Bell MP. Also on my London trip I wasn't allowed in Harrods – not because I'm a huge lion but because I was wearing shorts! Believe it or not I'm the only mascot to have held the Premiership trophy. The reason is a secret!

In the community...

I have my own children's charity – the Roary Club. Its president is Kirsty O'Brien and it raises money for special causes, including certain hospitals and schools.

Best thing about mascot life...

I have my own TV show on Boro TV NTL which goes out to thousands of people. It features soccer skills, questions to the players, and a certain quiz between children and teachers!

Thanks to Middlesborough FC, North News, and *Middlesbrough Evening Gazette*.

Playful Lion – Roary gets dizzy playing with his mates.

MANSFIELD TOWN
SAMMY THE STAG

MILLWALL
ZAMPA THE LION

Sammy has relatives in Sherwood Forest who can still be seen on the Mansfield Club crest. As well as being fast and athletic when he competes at mascot events, Sammy is popular at home with a sweet bucket and an accurate throw – mascots have highly evolved limbs for dispensing sweets and saving penalties!

With so many lion mascots it's hard to be different, but Zampa has a distinct name for starters (taken from the road outside the stadium) and has had a lion cub companion in recent years. Zampa starred on TV before Millwall's 2004 Cup Final appearance, and the 1927 Millwall lion might have been the first two-legged furball amongst the mascots.

Thanks to: Mansfield Town FC, Richard Parkes.

Thanks to: Millwall FC, Action Images.

Fighting with fire

When Northampton Town moved to the Sixfields Stadium along came a new arrival – a dragon mascot from the club crest. Legend has it that Clarence was hatched from an egg found by builders when they were digging foundations for the new ground. A similar thing happened at Highbury but Clarence is mythical, not from the Jurassic.

'Who are ya?'
CLARENCE THE DRAGON

What's your trademark?
I do a dragon picture-signature which the kids love for their autograph books.

Grand National finishing position?
Outside the top 10 yet, but wait till I get my wings working!

Favourite food
Knight Burgers – they're nice and crunchy with the armour left on!

Highlights of your career...
Appearing on the AXA FA Cup adverts. They showed that dragons are better mascots than dinosaurs! I was once fined by the FA for pushing a ref. I'm a bit more obedient these days though.

Elvis asks Clarence not to breathe on his hair.

In the community...
I enjoy meeting Clarence Club members, helping local charities, opening events, and I've been in pantomime – strangely enough, I played a dragon.

Worst thing about mascot life...
Getting my tail pulled. If only I could breathe fire backwards – that would put a stop to it!

Best thing about mascot life...
Entertaining kids and frightening referees!

Thanks to: Northampton Town FC, Pete Norton.

NORWICH CITY
CAPTAIN CANARY

Yellow Peril

The Dutch settlers of Norfolk bred canaries and the tradition was kept up in the county. It led to the football club's canary symbol and Canaries nickname. Now the giant mutant Captain Canary patrols Carrow Road with his moggie friend Splat the Cat.

'Who are ya?'
CAPTAIN CANARY

What's your trademark?

Me and Splat the Cat specialise in cartwheels. I'm also good at arithmetic, but I don't recommend doing maths on match days – I was once reported to the Football League for being cheeky in counting the small number of Wimbledon fans who's turned up at Carrow Road!

Interests outside football?

Cooking lessons – not from my girlfriend, Camilla Canary, but another fine lady linked with Norwich City!

Favourite food

I love Coleman's mustard and prefer it neat – it doesn't show if I spill any!

In the community...

I do lots of work for local charities and people with disabilities. It's a terrific job and makes a change from trying out Delia's recipes.

Word on the street about you...

Sophie Ellis-Bextor once said that the best thing about her visit to a match at Carrow Road was Captain Canary and Splat the Cat.

Thanks to: Norwich City FC, Roy Wiley, Will Hoy, and Roger Harris.

'Who are ya?'
MR AND MRS MAGPIE

Nicknames
We dont have any nicknames but people insist on calling us PENGUINS! How many striped penguins do you know? Or striped magpies for that matter!

How do you take penalties?
That's top secret – the coaching staff at Meadow Lane have taught us everything we know and that's not a lot!

Love of your life
Mrs Magpie: I'm a bit of a maneater and have got through three husbands in four years – Elizabeth Taylor eat your heart out!

Who do you need to get even with?
Mr Magpie: Floyd of Charlton Athletic – we had a mud-wrestle in the rain at Bolton's MascotMania event, and he started it.

Highlights of your career...
Mrs Magpie: I won the much coveted 'Ugliest Mascot' award at the 2002 Mascots Grand National. It takes pride of place in the Notts County trophy cabinet because it's the only thing in there!

In the community...
We like to raise money for good causes, even for our own club. Mrs Magpie once pinched Sherwood the Bear's head and auctioned it back to Nottingham Forest fans. It raised £200 for the Save Notts County fund.

Worst thing about mascot life...
Mr Magpie: I said that if we lost at Southport in the 2002 FA Cup I'd expose part of my anatomy. Silly me – we did lose and a select few were unlucky enough to see the sight!

Word on the street about you...
'Great looking penguins, aren't they?'

Thanks to: Empics, Notts County Supporters' Club.

Helping hand – Nottingham Forest striker David Johnson meets Mrs Magpie at Meadow Lane and donates £500 to the Save Notts County fund.

Calming the nerves – Mr and Mrs Magpie get ready for the 2003 Grand National

OLDHAM ATHLETIC
CHADDY THE OWL

The Oldham Express...

Chaddy is setting new standards in mascot speed. He broke the course record at the 2002 Huntingdon Grand National and returned to win it again in 2003. He's a firm favourite with the locals and the bookies.

'Who are ya?'
CHADDY THE OWL

What's in the name?
Chaddy is from the Chaddy End where the home fans sit, short for the Chadderton Road End.

What's your trademark?
A pitch-lengh run-up for a penalty kick and then a back heel. I once missed against Cardiff City and nearly hit the corner flag – the team went on to lose 7-1! Other Chaddy trademarks are blistering pace, and cartwheels. I once tried doing a handstand, not realising my hands didn't go higher than my ears, so my ears stuck in the ground and I nearly broke my neck and had to be stretchered off!

Grand National finishing position?
2000 – 3rd   2001 – 2nd   2002 – 1st   2003 – 1st
The secret's in the training and the porridge diet!

Highlights of your career
Winning the Mascot Grand National in 2002 after coming close in previous years. Ladbrokes paid out over £30,000 on me and didn't risk giving me long odds in 2003! I was once sent off for being repeatedly flagged offside in a match against Peterborough, when the linesman mistook me for a player. I did have the Oldham kit on but I've also got a big furry head! I once stood behind the net waving my wings trying to put Reading's Darren Caskey off taking a penalty. He missed, but the ref let him retake it. I received a warning letting from the FA!

Best thing about mascot life...
Putting smiles on people's faces. It gives you happiness that can't be measured. I also help the Make a Wish Foundation, Derian House Children's Hospice, Royal Oldham Hospital, Booth Hall Hospital, Children In Need and local schools to name but a few.

Thanks to: Oldham Athletic FC.

left: The velocity of fur – Chaddy charges home at the 2003 Grand National

Owl's perch – Chaddy looks a natural at the Grand National winning post.

OXFORD UTD
OLLIE THE OX

PETERBOROUGH UTD
PETER BURROW

'Who are ya?'
OLLIE THE OX

What's in the name?
The town of Oxford was based around a ford for oxen across a river. I'm an Ox and there aren't many names beginning with an O.

What's your trademark?
My floppy horn!

Grand National finishing position?
Mid-pack, but ahead of Rockin' Robin from Swindon.

Interests outside football?
Stud duties, standing in fields, and watching old videos of *Bullseye*.

Highlights of your career...
Appearing in this book!

Best mates
I hang out with lots of footballers: Steve Bull, Gordon Cowans, Lee Bullock...

Thanks to: Newsquest – Oxfordshire, Oxford United and Chris Williams.

'Who are ya?'
PETER BURROW

What's in the name?
It sounds like Peterborough doesn't it?

How do you take penalties?
Try and knock my opponent's head off!

Grand National finishing position?
2001 – 47th   2002 – 7th   2003 – 3rd

Highlights of your career...
Being petted by Page 3 girls at the Grand National. Hopefully they'll take me home for their hutch next year! Winning 'Midlands fastest mascot' at Leicester's Filbert Way in 2003. Being called 'smelly' by Helen Chamberlain on Soccer AM. Doesn't she know we all smell? She should try a whiff of her own Torquay Utd's Gilbert the Gull! I've helped out Children in Need and the Rudolph Foundation – a local charity which sends disadvantaged children to Disneyland in Paris.

Who do you need to get even with?
Bury's Robbie the Bobby for pulling off one of my ears!

Worst thing about mascot life...
The things our manager Barry Fry calls me when I get him in a headlock.

Best thing about mascot life...
Being expected to wind up people, and enjoying the experience!

Thanks to: *Peterborough Evening Telegraph*, Eric Daly, www.theposh.com.

Photo finish – Peter Burrow beat Sammy the Stag by a head in this 2003 race at Filbert Way.

PLYMOUTH ARGYLE
PILGRIM PETE

Following your faith

In 1620 the Pilgrim Fathers set sail from Plymouth to North America, hoping to settle in a land where they could follow their strict Puritan faith. After a three-month voyage to America they founded a new colony, calling it Plymouth, in Massachusetts. Pilgrim Pete is a symbol of those determined pilgrims. Pete has dropped anchor at Home Park so he can follow his own faith – footy and Plymouth Argyle.

'Who are ya?'
PILGRIM PETE

What's in the name?

The Pilgrim Fathers' ship, the *Mayflower*, forms our club emblem and our nickname is The Pilgrims.

Nickname

Pasty Pete! Yep, I'm fond of the local delicacy here.

Stepping out at Home Park – it's calmer than the ocean.

What's your trademark?

My massive moustache. I've got more whiskers than any other mascot – even Mighty Mariner! Also, I search out any hats of other teams that kids in the Plymouth section might be wearing. I confiscate the hats and throw them into the crowd. The kids seem to enjoy the treatment and bring the hats to me, risking never seeing them again.

Highlights of your career...

Slamming a penalty past Southend's Sammy the Shrimp at the AXA mascots' event at Wembley in 2000 (okay, so he's not the most agile goalie). Now Argyle have scored at both ends of Wembley stadium, following Ronnie Mauge's 1996 play-off winner against Darlington. Holding aloft the Division 3 championship trophy in 2002.

I'm always on hand to do charity and school events and I help out with the Junior Greens at Argyle.

Worst thing about mascot life...

First, having your head used as shooting practice by players and other mascots – and what with my towering Pilgrim's hat, I'm an easy target! And second, washing my moustache is quite a hassle!

Word on the street about you...

'You look like my wife!' – Former Plymouth manager Paul Sturrock on being introduced to Pilgrim Pete.

Thanks to: Plymouth Argyle FC, John Allen – *Evening Herald*.

Frog at Fratton – Frogmore appears from the damp corners of the ground…

Play up, Pompey – Barry Harris, the Portsmouth sailor, holds his board up to Pompey supporters at Tottenham's White Hart Lane in 1967. Note the wooden rattles in the crowd.

'Who are ya?'
FROGMORE

What's in the name?
Our Fratton Park ground is in Frogmore Road. I took over from Portsmouth's retired sea dog, Nelson, in 2002.

What's your trademark?
I am big, blue and have a wicked smile.

How do you take penalties?
Very well – considering I've got webbed feet!

Finest hour
Seeing Pompey promoted to the Premiership as champions in 2003. It was all my doing!

Highlights of your career
I visit hospitals, schools and anyone who wants me to help them out.

Worst thing about mascot life
The close season... no footy to hop around to.

Best thing about mascot life
The insects... tasty. Especially large mascot ones…

Thanks to: Portsmouth FC, Rosie Francis, Richard Owen.

PORT VALE
BOOMER THE DOG

'Who are ya?'
BOOMER

What's in the name?
The name originates from the fans' song 'Boom Boom'.

How do you symbolise your club?
I'm a Staffordshire Bull Terrier!

What's your trademark?
Cocking my leg against the goalpost.

Grand National finishing position?
Non-runner due to illness – my vet wouldn't let me run.

Interests outside football?
Fetching sticks, and sniffing around for a mate.

Best mate
Crewe's Gresty the Lion – he helps me pick up a scent!

Favourite food
Referees' legs, and there's a good supply of Hippo meat across town at Stoke City.

Who do you need to get even with?
Bob Taylor – he always used to give me grief when he played for West Brom.

In the community
I bound into schools and hospitals when I'm let of the leash.

Worst thing about mascot life...
Not being allowed to bury bones on the pitch.

Best thing about mascot life...
I'm a dog who doesn't need a licence!

Nothing but a hound dog…

Thanks to: Port Vale FC and The Sentinel (photos).

A dog's life at Vale Park – Boomer prefers his basket in the manager's office.

PRESTON NORTH END
DEEPDALE DUCK

'Who are ya?'
DEEPDALE DUCK

What's in the name?
Deepdale is the name of our ground and Duck because I'm a duck! I'm not the innocent lamb on the Preston club crest.

Age
I waddled into Deepdale from the local reservoir in 1993.

What's your trademark?
I'm a mischievous fowl, but try not to cross the line too much. I used to tease our Ground Safety Officer by annoying opposition players and officials. Nigel got a bit upset and often threatened to cook me! I'm used to the orange sauce jokes. I'm also known for looking after mascots' lost property – especially red tails.

How do you take penalties?
With my wings and webbed feet I'm better designed for saving penalties. I once damaged a knee when keeping goal and the club surgeon had to fit me for crutches!

Who do you need to get even with?
The Bees at Burnley. They think they're better because they're more agile, but like the hare and the tortoise, Deepdale Duck will have his day!

Highlights of your career...
Our League Cup second leg match against Blackburn at Deepdale in 2000. I distracted Tim Flowers, their goalie, as we scored in the 1-0 win. Shame we lost the first leg 6-0. Doing my diving goal celebrations with the players against Arsenal in the Cup in 1998 – we lost, but it was my dive that was splashed across the morning papers!

Best thing about mascot life
How many other ducks are known up and down the country and give autographs to adoring fans? It's a ponderful life!

Thanks to: Preston North End FC and *Lancashire Evening Post*.

QUEENS PARK RANGERS
JUDE THE CAT

'Who are ya?'
JUDE THE STADIUM CAT

What's in the name?
St Jude was the name of the club that became QPR in the 1880s. My nickname, Top Cat, comes from the TV cartoon character from the 1970s.

Age
I moved into Loftus Road in 1997. It beats the Shepherd's Bush alleyways.

What's your trademark?
At halftime at Loftus Road I go in goal for our 'Round the Pole' competition. Fans from different parts of the stadium try to beat me from the penalty spot after they run around a pole 10 times. They get hopelessly dizzy, so find it difficult to get a good strike of the ball. It all helps my reputation as goalkeeper No.1!

Grand National finishing position?
51st out of 85. I got distracted chasing too many birds on the course.

Interests outside football?
Keeping the stadium free of pigeons and keeping Ian Holloway's seat warm when he's not in the office. He doesn't know I sharpen my claws on his seat!

Favourite food
Canaries, magpies, robins and Elvis J Eel of Southend!

Highlights of your career...
Showing my goalkeeping prowess at Wembley against Portsmouth's Nelson the dog, then scoring past him in Geoff Hurst's World Cup winning goal, and finally lifting the FA Cup aloft. It looked great on the FA Cup TV adverts, and I dream that QPR will do it for real before I've had my nine lives! Starring in Channel 4's Banzai programme with Charlton's Floyd and Crystal Palace's Pete the Eagle. The day a cat, dog and eagle ran riot! I attend school events and do other work with local kids. Cats are generally lazy, but I love doing community work like this.

Best thing about mascot life...
Standing in front of the 'Loft' when the team comes out, and seeing the smiles on kids' faces! Makes me purr all over!

Thanks to: Queens Park Rangers FC.

Moggy in midfield –
Jude with QPR midfield star Marc Bircham.

'Who are ya?'
KINGSLEY ROYAL

What's in the name?
The club's nickname is the Royals, after a lion statue memorial to the Royals regiment in Reading town centre.

Age
I made my debut at Reading's old ground, Elm Park, in 1997. I now roam the grassy plains of the Madejski Stadium.

What's your trademark?
I'm great at keepy-uppies, and I'm known for my breakdancing, my spectacular goal celebrations, and my ability to attract the ladies.

How do you take penalties?
With ferocity – I went one season unbeaten!

Love of your life
Queensley of course! She stays in the den a lot so don't tell her about all the other females that stroke me on match days.

Favourite food
Pies, sweets, and Swindon fans!

Who do you need to get even with?
Swindon's Rockin' Robin – I had a shocker in a penalty shoot-out when we last met.

Worst thing about mascot life...
Territorial disputes – I've had them with Middlesbrough's Roary and with Wycombe's Bodger. I was sent off in 2002 against Cambridge Utd. It was for 'entering the field of play during the match' and I stopped the ball going out of touch! Well that ref should try my vision and see if he can tell where the touchline is!

Best thing about mascot life...
I'll always come out of the den to put smiles on fans' faces. Oh, and unconfined goal celebrations – Yeeesss!

Thanks to: Reading FC (photos).

Gizmo addiction – Kingsley holds a date to make all Reading fans proud – the 1871 formation of the club.

ROCHDALE
DESMOND THE DRAGON

'Who are ya?'
DESMOND THE DRAGON

Interests outside football?
Going to barbecues and producing firework displays.

Best mate
Halifax's Freddy the Fox – mind you, we had a little scrape in 1999 after he cocked his leg against our goal post. It all started as friendly pushing and shoving but then neither of us backed down.

Worst thing about mascot life...
It's hot and tiring – especially when I run out of puff!

Best thing about mascot life...
The kids love me, it gets me out of my cave, and I have my pick of the dragon dollies! I give presents to children in hospital at Christmas, I attend parties and get to open events.

Word on the street about you...
'I wish our 'keeper could save penalties like him!' – Rochdale Manager

Thanks to: Rochdale FC, Empics (photo).

Fluffy and scaly – Desmond out of his cave at Spotland.

ROTHERHAM UTD
DUSTY MILLER

'Who are ya?'
DUSTY MILLER

What's in the name?
The Millers is Rotherham United's nickname and Dusty Miller is a well known local hostelry.

Sponsor
Papa Luigi's Italian restaurant. My nickname is Chewy.

What's your trademark?
I've got one of the biggest heads amongst the mascots and have to take care not to topple over in the Grand National. Perhaps more pizza would make me less top heavy.

In the community...
I do various functions, and especially like to help the MacMillan Appeal and the NSPCC.

Thanks to: Rotherham Utd FC.

Clinging on to their youth – Dusty invites his mates round.

RUSHDON & DIAMONDS
DAZZLER THE LION

Dazzler is enjoying life in the Football League as Rushden look the part at their impressive Nene Park ground. Dazzler became an overnight star in 2001 when he won the Mascot Grand National, following the withdrawal of Olympic hurdler Matthew Douglas as Freddie the Fox. Dazzler was a rank outsider for that piece of silverwear, but his second place eventually won him the title when Freddie withdrew – see the Grand National section for full details. Few mascots have knocked the speed merchant Chaddy the Owl off his perch, but Dazzler kept out of trouble and proved Chaddy can be beaten.

Thanks to: Rushden and Diamonds FC, Empics.

SCUNTHORPE UTD
SCUNNY BUNNY

The steel mills around Scunthorpe's Glanford Park give rise to the club's nickname 'The Iron'. It's not ideal territory for rabbits, but in 1998 the cotton-tailed Scunny Bunny arrived at the club. He's a popular sight behind the goal and helps his club take football to the community. He's not far from another member of his clan – Peter Burrow across the fens at Peterborough. But with rumours of Peter turning into a griffin, scunny will soon be head of the warren.

Thanks to: Scunthorpe United FC.

Iron's Bunny – Scunny takes a break from the carrot juice.

SHEFFIELD UNITED
CAPTAIN BLADE

Nerves of steel

Long hours at sea have done strange things to Captain Blade – he plays sea shanties on his saxophone! The Captain is popular amongst other mascots but if they don't like his jokes he can brandish his swords and make them walk the plank!

'Who are ya?'
CAPTAIN BLADE

What's in the name?
The Blades' nickname comes from Sheffield's once-great steel industry, and I wield the crossed swords of the club crest.

How do you take penalties?
Actually I'm a goalkeeper – 'Fingers Blade' – so I prefer to stop penalties, which I'm good at even without my swords.

Grand National finishing position?
Don't ask – I'm better at sea than on land!

Interests outside football?
I trade in Sheffield steel cutlery up and down the oceans.

Finest hour
Bowling over arch-rival Ozzie Owl at the Owlerton speedway stadium. A little old owl is no match for a pirate and his parrot!

Best mate
Captain Pugwash. I'm also acquainted with our local MP – he was made Minister of Sport despite knowing me!

Who do you need to get even with?
City Gent – he nicks all my jokes and tricks!

Worst thing about mascot life...
Sweating, and too many groupies!

Best thing about mascot life...
Helping Weston Park Hospital and the NSPCC, and seeing kids' faces at the ground when they meet a mild-mannered pirate like me!

Thanks to: Sheffield United FC and Andy Dakin.

SHEFFIELD WEDNESDAY
OZZIE THE OWL, OLLIE AND BAZ

Three Wise Owls?

Hillsborough has three noisy chattering owls. Ozzie started as a cartoon way back in 1967 and changed to the real furry thing in 1992. He was later joined by his nephew, Ollie, and teenage tearaway, Bazz, with his baseball cap. The three owls have Donald Duck type twittery voices – it's a weird talent for mascots, so maybe they should do a turn with their fans' famous orchestra!

'Who are ya?'
OZZIE, OLLIE, AND BAZZ.

What's in the name?
As owls we represent the club's famous nickname and symbol, which comes from the Owlerton area of Sheffield.

Best mate
We should really be having him for breakfast, but we keep on good terms with our neighbour Chester the Fieldmouse.

Highlights of your career
Ozzie: For me it was my debut against Kaiserslauten in the UEFA Cup in 1992, and then going four (yes four!) times to Wembley in 1993. We love opening fairs and fêtes, and visiting local hospitals. We had a great time at the opening of the FA Premier League's Hall of Fame in London. It all gives the mice at Hillsborough a chance to recover!

Worst thing about mascot life...
Having squabbles in public with your relatives!

Best thing about mascot life...
Having squabbles in public with your relatives (hee hee)!

Thanks to: Steve Chu, Sheffield Wednesday FC.

SHREWSBURY TOWN
LENNY THE LION AND MRS LENNY

Lurking in the meadow

On April Fools' Day 2001, Mr and Mrs Lenny hosted an epic mascots' match in front of 3,500 fans at Gay Meadow. The Shrewsbury lions' team cruised to victory and Channel 4 screened the highlights (look out for Elvis J Eel's report on the match elsewhere in this book). Later in 2001 Lenny was voted mascot of the year for his great work in the mascot world.

Lenny starred on Match of the Day in 2003, displaying a giant Everton mint he'd made for Everton's FA Cup third-round visit to Gay Meadow. He even sailed the FA Cup across the river in his coracle that day – he and the trophy stayed afloat, but Everton didn't!

Mrs Lenny represents Shrewsbury Town Women's and Girls' Football Club, who these days are probably a match for the lads.

Thanks to: Mathew Ashton and Empics, Gary Bright, Shrewsbury Town FC, Shrewsbury Town Women's and Girls' FC, Natalie Brown.

A drop of rain! Shrewsbury's Lenny the Lion paddles in the club's coracle as Gay Meadow is flooded in 2000. The day's match against Kidderminster was called off!

Saintly St Bernards

Sammy and Super do plenty of charity work and once helped *Blue Peter* with a bikeathon. In 2003, Super was given dancing lessons live on TV before the FA Cup Final. His companion was another creature hardly known for his graceful movement – Gunnersaurus!

'Who are ya?'
SUPER SAINT AND SAMMY SAINT

What's your trademark?
Sammy: I'm a bouncy young pup who likes to be outrageously naughty when I can manage it, and Super balances a football on his nose.

Interests outside football?
Super: Chasing cats and walkies.
Sammy: Kennel Club.

Finest hour
Super: Saving a penalty from our former keeper Paul Jones.
Sammy: Scoring a penalty past Stamford the Lion at Wembley.

Who do you need to get even with?
Sammy: The policeman who once tripped me up in front of the entire crowd!
Super: Frogmore, because he's from Portsmouth!

Best thing about mascot life...
Not being scolded when we're disobedient!

Thanks to: Southampton FC, and Paul Collins – *Daily Echo* (photo).

Saints go Marching… Super Saint with the fans at the 2003 FA Cup semi-final.

SOUTHEND UNITED
ELVIS J EEL AND SAMMY THE SHRIMP

How d'you like your seafood?

Elvis and Sammy are seafood legends who surfaced from the Thames estuary. Elvis likes strumming his inflatable guitar and twitching his jellied eel ears, while Sammy just tries to avoid getting his head bent. Never tempted to eat each other, they make Southend's seaside barmy as well as balmy!

'Who are ya?'
ELVIS J EEL

Nickname
The King of Mascots or the Tweenie Wannabe!

What's your trademark?
I am royalty so I always have to look good. I even comb my hair between taking penalties.

Elvis avoids giving Sammy any headers.

Grand National finishing position?
2001 – 108th I caused that massive forty-mascot pile up!
2002 – around 20th, but the event was marred by disaster when my hair got blown out of place!

Who do you need to get even with?
I am the King so everyone looks up to me. Saying that, Broxi Bear from Rangers knocked me out of the Disney Channel Mascot Cup, and my neighbours Eddie the Eagle and Theo the Wyvern both smell!

Highlights of your career...
I'm a frequent visitor to Southend Hospital. I'm always opening shops and doing things for our community, and I'm hoping to launch a ship one day! Finally, there was an incident with plastic pants at Bolton's Reebok Stadium, but you'll have to ask Captain Blade about that! The photo has been censored from this book!

Best thing about mascot life...
Being with the fans, putting smiles on faces, enjoying the freedom on the pitch... wow, I'd pinch myself if I could feel anything!

'Who are ya?'
SAMMY THE SHRIMP

What's in the name?
Us being Seasiders and well... the sea! We're also nicknamed the Shrimpers.

Nickname
Conehead, amongst other unmentionable things.

What's your trademark?
Finishing last in the Mascot Grand National every year and just being a legend!

Interests outside football
Rockpooling, and wriggling along the pier.

Highlights of your career
Dating Kylie was probably the highlight, followed closely by being voted 'Ugliest Mascot' in 2001.

Favourite food
Funnily enough I quite like eels.

The Legend of Sammy the Shrimp

Before the pink version of Sammy, the character in the 1980s was a really naff design, being ugly and unconvincing. At the end of one season the costume was put to rest in a store cupboard while renovation work went on at Roots Hall. Completely forgotten about, it emerged for the first time in nearly a decade during the 1997-98 campaign. This costume was a joke amongst home and away fans and was widely known as 'Johnny'. In the 1998-99 season the local paper ran a competition to see who could design a new mascot shrimp. The winning design was brought to life and became the next Sammy.

Around 8 feet tall, Sammy's rigid and luminous pink costume restricted each pace to a hobble but he completed four Grand Nationals and even escorted Sun model Lelani to the finishing line. Coming last has its rewards and is now fiercely contested each year at Huntingdon.

Sammy the Shrimp is so silly that he's acquired cult status, and that explains why a fan paid £400 for the old pink costume at an auction. He's become a legend alongside other household names like Wolfie and Cyril. They are strong, wild and macho, he is cumbersome, daft and awkward – a surreal creature from the deep.

Thanks to: Southend Utd Commercial Dept, Robin Duncan, Ben Duncan and Trevor Benbrook.

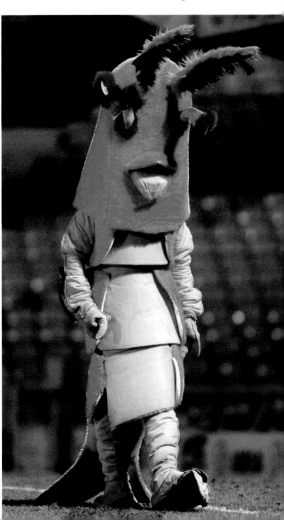

The limping legend – the 8ft fluorescent shrimp squirms along the touchline...

STOCKPORT COUNTY
VERNON BEAR

'Who are ya?'
VERNON BEAR

What's in the name?
I was found on Edgeley train station on 1 April 1996 by my sponsor, the Vernon Building Society in Stockport.

How do you symbolise your club?
I'm as mad as a hatter!

What's your trademark?
Dancing to the theme tune of the 'Hair Bear Bunch' and playing invisible tennis.

Finest hour
Getting a standing ovation at Maine Road from the loyal County fans.

In the community...
I especially like to help Marie Curie Cancer Research.

Worst thing about mascot life.
I'm always on the pitch but never get a game.

Word on the street about you...
'It was reported that the mascot was going to retire. That would be like selling Luke Beckett. This is your home Vernon – don't go' – *Walter Pickford*, season ticket holder for 22 years.

Thanks to: Stockport County FC.

Warm-up at Edgeley Park – Vernon heads for the woods

STOKE CITY
POTTERMUSS AND POTTERMISS

Hippos amongst the china
The china and porcelain products made in Stoke and the surrounding Potteries can be found on dining tables and in homes across the world. Pottermus and Pottermiss are proud of the area's great industrial tradition and are in their element on grass, mud or clay.

'Who are ya?'
POTTERMUS AND POTTERMISS

What's in the name?
Stoke City are the Potters from the Potteries, so we are hippo potters!

Age
Pottermus arrived in Stoke in 1998 and met Pottermiss in a nearby swamp in 2002.

What's your trademark?
Pottermus: My striking poses – easy with a body like mine!
Pottermiss: Jigging along to our fans' theme tune – Tom Jones' song 'Delilah'!

Highlights of your career...
Pottermus: Being the mystery guest on TV's They Think it's all Over – good job I'm not ticklish!
Pottermiss: The welcome I got when I arrived at the Britannia Stadium – they needed a lady around the place!

Best thing about mascot life...
It's warm, hot and sticky – perfect for hippos!

Thanks to: Stoke City FC and *The Sentinel*.

90

How do you take penalties?
Sadly I take penalties like a girl (my claws are delicate, you know). I sometimes lie in front of the opponent rubbing my tail to put them off.

Highlights of your career...
Appearing on Sky TV conducting an orchestra at the Stadium of Light. I copied the conductor who then let me take over. I then found my tail made a better baton and carried on while members of the orchestra were desperately trying not to crease up with laughter. I'm reliably informed that the punters in the Sky studio were rolling about too!

Snatching a red-and-white pom-pom from a cheerleader at Sheffield United – well they're our colours too! At the photo-shoot in the centre circle she started screaming at me, much to the entertainment of our fans. She smacked me on my head before I gave it back. But where there's no sense there's no feeling!

'Who are ya?'
SAMSON

What's in the name?
We're the black cats from the club's nickname. Our previous sponsors, Vaux Breweries, have a brand of beer called Samson.

Interests outside football?
I'm really busy with my eating and sleeping, but try and fit in some dancing, abseiling, parachuting and fun running – the usual feline stuff.

Highlights of your career...
Winning the Mascot Challenge in Trafalgar Square in 2001.

I do school and community visits through our junior supporters' club, and have done fun-runs and parachute jumps. It makes a change from sleeping!

Abseiling from the huge Wearmouth and Tyne Bridges – cats always land on their feet!

'Who are ya?'
DELILA

What's your trademark?
My 'girlie' walk – a confident, slinky prowl to attract Samson, who's easily distracted by glamorous women. I also creep up behind people and put the tip of my tail in their ear, which they keep swatting away, thinking it's a fly. Eventually they turn round and get a big fright!

SUNDERLAND
THE BLACK CATS – SAMSON AND DELILA

Best thing about mascot life...

My extra catting jobs include helping with Comic Relief, visits to local hospitals, and children's party. I also have close connections with a school in that unmentionable place, (Newcastle)

I've made lots of friends amongst the young fans, some of which are very special (Hi Josh!).

Thanks to: Ed Cook, Nigel Connah, Rob Mason, Tony Davison, Anthony Stephenson, Allan Swan, Ross Duncan, North News (photo of Samson), Two Can Design, Action Images.

'Who are ya?'
CYRIL THE SWAN

A swan, a legend, a celebrity...

In the world of mascots they don't come any bigger than Cyril the Swan. Dubbed 'Mascot No.1', he's the David Beckham of the furballs. He's the one the kids swarm around at mascot events, who gets mobbed in the streets of his home town Swansea, and who attracts the media in his every move. Why is Cyril such a draw? How has this particular mascot, among all others, become as big as his club?

The legend is born

Cyril arrived at Swansea's Vetch Field in 1998. His debut was spectacular – when the fanfare finished he really did descend from the floodlights – the crowd roared their approval and Cyril was an instant hit. The fans wanted a prankster – a lively swan, pounding up and down the touchline and loitering behind the goal. They got all that and more. Cyril was brave, cheeky and feisty.

Wings clipped

The early days of Cyril saw a great cup run for lowly Swansea. Stoke, Millwall and West Ham were despatched with heroic displays. With each giant-killing goal the number one fan just couldn't contain himself – he charged onto the pitch, leaping for joy amongst the celebrating players. The cameras followed his reaction to every Swansea raid on goal. Telly audiences were watching a mascot as much as the edited highlights. He was as gripping as the goal-mouth scrambles.

But then it all stopped. In the following season's cup the Swans were knocking in goals at home against Millwall. True to form, out of the traps came Cyril, hurtling onto the pitch, his wings aloft in delight. But this time it was different. The ref on the day took exception to the passionate swan. He reported the incident to the Welsh FA. The celebrating swan was bringing the game into disrepute, claimed the ref.

Grace and elegance – the flying swan.

SWANSEA CITY
CYRIL THE SWAN

above: The scrum for Cyril – The giant swan faces the media in 1999 after the Welsh FA announce his touchline ban at Swansea.

below: Don't lose your heads guys! Just a friendly jostle between Cyril and Millwall's Zampa? Moments after this photo the lion's head did get lost, and was found in the crowd.

Paul Merton speaks out

The news of a nine-foot swan facing a disciplinary committee didn't go unnoticed. On BBC's *Have I Got news for You* comedian Paul Merton asked what the world was coming to if a giant swan couldn't celebrate his own team's success. Cyril got letters of support from other mascots like Shrewsbury's Lenny the Lion, and even his archrival Bartley the Bluebird (now RIP) at Cardiff City. Two national papers launched campaigns to defend Cyril's antics, and Swansea were bombarded with fans' support for their hero.

A mute swan in the dock

In April 1999 it happened – Cyril was hauled in front of the three-man commission at the Welsh FA and faced his charges. The club chairman was present to support his case, and to interpret the swan's body language to the puzzled men in suits. After the hour-long hearing, Cyril was banished from the touchline and the club fined £1,000. Swansea apologised, Cyril was reported to be sorry, and the club said they'd build him a nest in the corner of the ground. Cyril had once more put Swansea in the limelight, and his fame spread further.

Legends team up…
Cyril meets H'Angus – what are they up to?

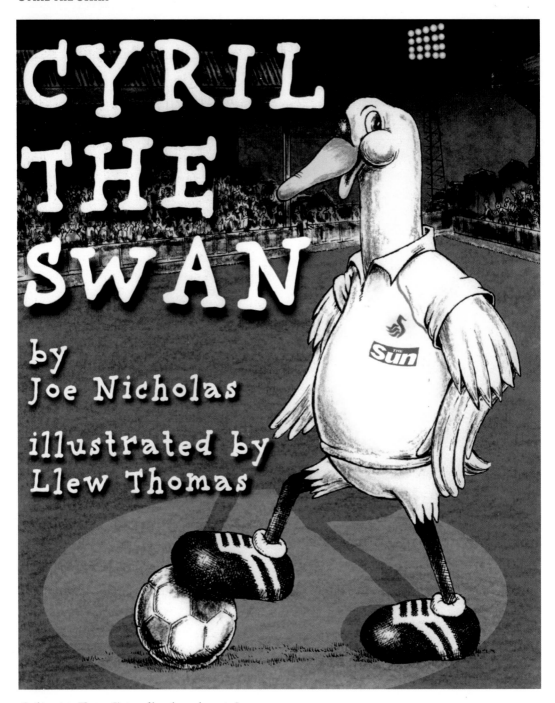

CYRIL THE SWAN

by Joe Nicholas

illustrated by Llew Thomas

Cyril in print – The true (?) story of how the rascal came to Swansea

'Nice Swan Cyril'

Cyril's celebrity status makes for a hectic life. His adventures described below have ranged from pantomime to politics…

Webbed-footed performance

In his first season he made a CD recording for Christmas – 'Nice Swan Cyril'. It was a sell-out in the club shop, even though his mates had to sing while he cavorted to the music – it's tricky being mute and singing solo! He's also been a star of the stage, having appeared in the Christmas panto, Aladdin, at Swansea's Grand Theatre. He played the Emperor of China's pet, and had no problems with stage fright!

Cyril is constantly booked for all manner of functions. His commitments include shop openings, charity events, parties and wedding appearances. He's even shown his respect at a fan's funeral.

Wing Play

At the Mascot Grand National Cyril is usually too busy having a good time to worry about the glory of victory. But in the second National in 2000 he did prove his mettle. He kept his neck down and flew to the finish, grabbing third spot, and bringing back Wales' first medal from the event. Cyril is a nifty footballer too – in a North v. South mascots' match at Derby's Pride Park in 2002, Cyril got the winner for the South with a twenty-yard screamer past Captain Blade of Sheffield United – it was some curtain-raiser for the Queen's Jubilee visit to the stadium!

Ruling the roost

He's already a household name, but Cyril still has lofty ambitions. He applied for the England manager's job in October 2000 when Sven was appointed. He claimed he was a good motivator (he's not nicknamed 'Psycho' for nothing) and had the perfect body language to fire up the players from the dugout. Whether he could stop himself straying from the manager's area is another matter. Not put off by the rejection, he's hinted at running for the Welsh Assembly, and has pledged to share the generous salary with the club.

Flying high

What's left for the mighty Swan to conquer? Not a lot really. There's already been a TV show on his life at Swansea, and he's been voted No.1 mascot in *Match of the Day Magazine*, where he beat off the hordes of Man United fans' backing Fred the Red. He's even drawn the Saturday night National Lottery, being star attraction in the 'Your number's up' show. If mascots got transfers Cyril would be linked with the Premiership elite, or a glamour club amongst Europe's finest. But Cyril is above all that – he knows he's top of football's real pecking order!

Special thanks to: Phil Rees, Martin Ellard, www.dragon-pictures.com, James Davies, *Western Mail and Echo*, Christopher Davies Publishers Ltd, Llew Thomas.

SWINDON TOWN
ROCKIN ROBIN

SWINDON TOWN F.C.

Rocket Robin!

Swindon Town were once known as the Railwaymen – the station was a hub for the old Great Western steam trains which rattled through. Today, it's Rockin Robin's penalties that rocket past you at the County Ground, as all his furry opponents will testify! He's deadly from the spot and hasn't lost a shoot-out yet – err, don't we need him for England?

'Who are ya?'
ROCKIN' ROBIN

What's your trademark?
My pre-match dance – Swindon's version of the Hakka!

Grand National finishing position?
2001 – 9th
2002 – 45th, but ruthlessly tripped by a stray boot when I was in contention. They even showed me going down on ITN News, such was the enormity of the event!

Interests outside football?
Line dancing – keeps me in shape for my pre-match Hakka. Extreme ironing (that's ironing in crazy places, like on top of the floodlights) – keeps me composed and ice cool for my penalties!

Who do you need to get even with?
Oxford's Ollie the Ox for slurring my name in the paper – watch your back Ollie!

Highlights of your career...
Scoring a brace in a mascots' match at Bolton, then being red-carded by John McGinlay. The red card was more fun!

I do school fêtes, hospital visits and lots of charity fundraising. Great to see the children's faces when I meet them!

Worst thing about mascot life...
On the last day of the 2001/02 season there was a pitch invasion at the end of the game. I stood in front of the goalmouth behind some stewards. Suddenly around thirty big blokes ran at them – the stewards scattered and I got beaten up. My boots were stolen but the police recovered them and made arrests, while all I got was a bruised wing!

Best thing about mascot life...
Hearing the crowd roar my name and being mascot for the best team in England – well, best in Wiltshire anyway!

In memory of Jimmy Davis: As this book was in preparation we learnt of the tragic death of Jimmy Davis, pictured in the photo with Rockin' Robin. Jimmy was with Manchester United, Swindon and then Watford and looking forward to a bright career. He was much liked at Swindon Town and will be greatly missed.

Thanks to: Swindon Town FC .

'Who are ya?'
GILBERT THE GULL

What's in the name?
I was created in the 1960s by a local journalist and was known as Gulliver, then changed to Gilbert in the mid-1980s. I've no idea why the name changed so if anyone out there knows then please get in touch.

Nickname
It's not printable – I only hear it behind my back.

Sponsors
I'm honoured to have two: Torbay Council, and our supporters' club, Capital Gulls.

How do you symbolise your club?
I'm a seagull from the seaside of Torquay. I wear blue and yellow which represents the sand, sea and blue sky – not that we get much!

What's your trademark?
Yellow, webbed feet, a big beak, and an enormous white bum!

How do you take penalties?
Put the goalie off by making the goal line slippery – I can't tell you what with, but it's white!

Grand National finishing position?
I hope to be in the medal placings one day, and my large beak could be a clincher in a photo-finish.

Love of your life
Athena from neighbouring Exeter. Like Romeo and Juliet we are from opposite camps, so pretend to dislike each other – it's tough!

Favourite food
I pinch fish and chips from unsuspecting tourists, but Plainmoor's pasties are the best!

Who do you need to get even with?
I don't like the smart alec who invented Wheely bins – no more bin liners to rip apart!

In the community...
I help the council in their 'don't feed the gulls' campaign aimed at holidaymakers. How come I still need to watch my waistline then?

Worst thing about mascot life...
My beak doesn't open wide enough to sup pints!

Best thing about mascot life...
All gulls cause havoc at the seaside, but I'm the only one who's really allowed to.

Word on the street about you...
'It was a choice between a seagull or a bucket of sand – we felt a seagull was slightly more photogenic!' – *Mike Bateson* – chairman and owner of the club, when asked why a seagull was chosen as mascot.

Thanks to: Richard Hughes, Mike Bateson, Derek Hore, Kate Stevens, and Capital Gulls.

TOTTENHAM HOTSPUR
CHIRPY

Cockerel on his perch

Spurs' link with the cockerel symbol starts with the club's name of Hotspur, which gave rise to the nickname Spurs. It's thought that the cockerel was adopted as a symbol due to its fighting spurs. The cockerel motif first appeared on the playing kit for the 1921 FA Cup final and has appeared on the shirts ever since. The cockerel and ball first appeared in 1909 when former player William James Scott cast a copper statue to perch on the then-new West Stand.

'Who are ya?'
CHIRPY

What's in the name?
I'm fun, happy, lucky, charming, handsome and well... er, chirpy.

Nickname
Chirp, Big Bird, Cocky.

How do you symbolise your club?
I bring fun, laughter, and happiness. However, my motto is: 'Walk with caution through the Cockerel's lair!'

How do you take penalties?
Who cares about penalties? I'm an entertainer, not an athlete! I'm not a bad keeper though.

Grand National finishing position?
I was pushing for a medal position in 2003 so watch out – the rooster's in his stride.

Interests outside football?
Keeping my plumage in good condition.

Highlights of your career...
Our Worthington Cup win at Wembley, and just the pleasure of pulling on the white shirt of Spurs. I visit hospitals and schools and as many children as I can.

Best thing about mascot life...
Walking down the tunnel out onto the White Hart lane pitch... then entertaining the fans and families, and being loved by all the ladies!

Thanks to: Andy Porter, Tottenham Hotspur FC, Action Images.

'Who are ya?'
ROVER

What's your trademark?

I walk around the stands and throw a ball into the crowd and it gets headed back – people of all ages join in, even the stewards.

As I pass out sweets and meet people the kids know that I want good behavious from them, and that's what i get.

How do you take penalties?

I use the 'Aldo shuffle' technique – sending the keeper the wrong way like Rovers star John Aldridge used to do.

Highlights of your career

I once carried a lad out of his wheelchair to take a penalty. I held him tightly while he struck the ball, and he got a mighty roar from the crowd as the ball hit the net. As I carried him back he got a standing ovation, and he was both crying and laughing with delight.

A ref once told the two captains before kick off that my boots were better than theirs. They thought he was joking but I reckon he was right – I take pride in my boots and insist on the best, and I certainly don't risk big comic boots on our steps at the stadium.

It's funny how the lads in the crowd just want an autograph but the girls like Rover to hang around. I don't know what it is, but Rover has a certain appeal to them. It's all part of the magic of a mascot.

Best thing about mascot life...

Shaking hands with so many people and seeing happy children's faces. I like to raise money for good causes, including Macmillan Nurses and the children's hospice Zoe's Place.

Thanks to: Tranmere Rovers FC, and Chris Sumner, chief photographer, Wirral Globe (photo).

Goodie bag – Rover hands out sweets at Prenton Park, sponsored by friends Bryan and Mike in the crowd.

WALSALL
SWIFTY

'Who are ya?'
SWIFTY

What's in the name?
The swift is the emblem of Walsall FC, following our formation from the Walsall Swifts. One of the club's nicknames is the Swifts. The club crest has the international leather symbol together with the swift.

What's your trademark?
I do a skidding dive into the goalmouth before every game.

Swifty at home at the Bescot Stadium.

How do you take penalties?
Right foot folllowed by a dive skidding along the floor if I score (if I don't score, well, it saves on the washing).

Interests outside football?
I play in a rock'n'roll band – honest!

Finest hour
When Walsall got to the play-off final at the Millenium Stadium to play Reading. It was fantastic to get the fans cheering before the game in such a massive stadium!

Who do you need to get even with?
Rockin Robin from Wrexham (although he's now been laid off and replaced by Wrex the Dragon). He once jumped me from behind and my head came off – it's difficult to navigate when you're headless.

Charity and local community work ...
I give special help to the Allsports charity at Bloxwich in Walsall. I also make guest appearances for other local charities and good causes.

Best thing about mascot life
I represent my favourite football team and lead them onto the pitch at every home game – can't beat it, even in a rock 'n' roll band!

Thanks to: David Linney, Gemma Partridge, and Dougie Swain.

'Who are ya?'
HARRY THE HORNET

What's in the name?
I bring the club's nickname to life. I joined the swarm at Vicarage Road in 1995, and I buzz along the touchline swinging my stinger!

How do you take penalties?
With stinging precision.

Grand National finishing position?
I won the second Grand National and Harriet my wife came second the following year.

Who do you need to get even with?
Chaddy the Owl for temporarily looking after my Grand National title. Oh, and Happy Harry from Luton – local rivalry, can't beat it!

Highlights of your career...
The 1999 Wembley Division One play-off final. And we'll soon be back in the Prem! I help the club's football in the community events, ranging from holiday courses and after-school events to sessions for our friends with disabilities.

Worst thing about mascot life...
Losing races to your wife!

Best thing about mascot life...
The adulation, and being associated with the best community club in the land.

Word on the street about you...
'Do I like that Hornet!' – ex-manager *Graham Taylor*

'Mama Mia – wot-a pasta' as Arry been on? He-a moves-a so well.' – ex-manager *Gianluca Vialli*

'An inspiration to fans, players and staff alike.' – *Ray Lewington*

Thanks to: Watford FC, and Rob Howarth – Alban Donohoe Picture Service (Grand National photo).

WEST BROMWICH ALBION
BAGGIE BIRD AND JNR

Throstles at the Hawthorns

Baggie and Junior come from the old club nickname and the present-day club symbol, the Throstles. Throstle is the Black Country word for thrush. The club's ground was built on a site containing hawthorn bushes, and thrushes would have fed there. The Baggies is now the main nickname, and probably originates from the baggy trousers of steel and metalworkers in the early 1900s, when they came to matches straight from a Saturday-morning shift. Another possibility is that the gateman carrying money bags to the main office during each match got labelled as 'the baggies' by the onlooking crowd.

'Who are ya?'
BAGGIE BIRD AND JUNIOR BAGGIE

Baggie Bird wears the home kit of blue and white and Junior Baggie wears the away kit, which is usually yellow and green.

Family squabble? Baggie Bird and Junior limber up.

What's your trademark?
We do a forward roll over a football and launch it into the crowd. We're known for our UK hip-hop dancing – it gets the crowd pumped up before kick-off and is now part of the Hawthorns' experience.

How do you take penalties?
Well and very well! We don't have golden boots for nothing!

Grand National finishing position?
23rd and 28th in 2002 – change the subject quickly...

How will you improve next year?
Run faster! We can't be tops at everything, surely?

Interests outside football?
Birdwatching – The Hawthorns was a bird habitat after all.

In the community...
We do lots of charity and local community work, especially for Macmillan Nurses and for Children in Need.

Highlights of your career
At our home game against Crystal Palace in 2002 we needed a victory to clinch our first recent promotion to the Premiership. Manager Gary Megson told us to stay behind the goal all match to keep the fans vocal. The crowd responded and roared on the team. The players responded with a 2-0 win, and we were up. Afterwards we joined the players' party in the dressing room and Gary Megson said: 'You're as much a part of this club as the players'.

Thanks to: WBA FC, Tony Matthews.

Iron icons

West Ham take their Hammers nickname from the Thames Ironworks which built ships, bridges and other structures nearby on the banks of the river Thames. West Ham United itself emerged from the former Thames Ironworks FC in 1900. Sturdy hammers were crucial for nailing the rivets into structures at the ironworks, so the crossed hammers have been a central part of the club's crest.

The club is now just as famous for its theme song 'I'm Forever Blowing Bubbles'. The song was written in America and first sang at West Ham in the mid-1920s, when school friends watched their hero, 'Bubbles' Murray play for West Ham boys. Young Mr Murray had striking blond hair and resembled the lad in a Pears soap advert of the time. The bubbles connection came from that and the song soon caught on around the crowd.

Today, Herbie the Hammer and Bubbles the Bear are great heroes at Upton Park as they meet supporters, promote the club, and dance with the Hammerette cheerleaders.

They starred in a BBC documentary which explained their duties for the club, and they're clever critters too – Herbie has helped the club start a series of children's books, so now you can read all about their adventures in mascot world.

Thanks to: John Hellier (club info), Empics (photos).

Heavy machinery –
Herbie the Hammer looks for rivets at Upton Park.

Bubbly bundle –
Bubbles the Bear soaks up the match-day atmosphere.

WOLVERHAMPTON WANDERERS
WOLFIE AND WENDY

'Who are ya?'
WOLFIE

What's your trademark?
Pulling a moony at my fans, and a bit of banter with them – they just go wild, like me!

How do you take penalties?
Get the fans behind me chanting. Take three steps back, and clap my fans. Run… kick… and watch the ball hit the back of the net – yes!

Love of your life
Wendy Wolf – she is my rock. No other woman for me!

Favourite food
I'm no chef, so if it doesn't go 'ping' and take five minutes, Wolfie doesn't eat it. I do hunt pigs though…

Who do you need to get even with?
The three Pigs who met me at Bristol City in 1998. They'd better watch their mouths – no one winds up Wolfie and gets away with it!

Highlights of your career…
I made it into the *News of the World* and onto BBC's *Cup Final Grandstand* for my celebration of Nathan Blake's wonder goal in our 2003 cup run.

In the community…
Kids often take penalties against me to raise funds for their school or charity. Wolfie will always help his pack.

Best thing about mascot life…
My junior Wolves are behind me all the way – a fantastic feeling. 'WE ARE THE WOLVES!'

Call of the wild!

'Who are ya?'
WENDY WOLF

What's your trademark?
Distracting the opposition mascot to help Wolfie guard our patch.

How do you take penalties?
Apply my lipstick. Style my hair and bow. Slip and fall over on my bum. Leave it to Wolfie – he's the penalty king!

Grand National finishing position?
In the 2001 race I was pushed over twice by one of the Harlequin mascots and I'm still waiting for an apology! Oh, and Wolfie knows about this by the way!

Interests outside football?
Both Wolfie and I are great entertainers for parties and weddings and we love to see people laugh and smile at us.

Highlights of your career...
Doing a documentary for Channel 4 on being a female mascot – it was great fun! Also spending a day at Wembley with loads of other mascots filming adverts – brilliant! Being on the pitch with the players and meeting the fans is a highlight every time!

In the community
Although I'm really wild I also try to be a cuddly wolf and kids love me to bits. We do lots of events and help raise funds for charity – I'm even planning on a marathon for charity – hope there's some pigs to chase!

Best thing about mascot life...
Being close to the fans – they're great! Wolfie and Wendy are the Wolves! Gold and black through and through!

Thanks to: Wolverhampton Wanderers and Andy Morgan.

WIGAN ATHLETIC
JJ AND B

'Who are ya?'
JJ AND B

What's in the name?
Our main sponsor is JJB Sports – okay, it's not subtle but it's easy to remember!

How do you symbolise your club?
Latics is a family club and we are the figureheads of the North Stand family enclosure. We love children and they love us!

How do you take penalties?
JJ: It's my forte – I'm part of the club's strike force.

Finest Hour
Winning the Division Two championship in 2003.

Best mates
Bob the Builder, who's been to see us at Wigan, and an even bigger star – Chaddy the Owl!

Who do you need to get even with?
JJ: I fell out with Bloomfield Bear of Blackpool, and I don't think he's that keen on me – sorry I broke your tail Bloomfield, we must make it up sometime.

Thanks to: Wigan Athletic FC.

WREXHAM
WREX THE DRAGON

'Who are ya?'
WREX THE DRAGON

Nickname
I can't tell you what our assistant manager calls me!

Age
I started life at the Racecourse Ground in 2001, but I was a big baby!

How do you take penalties?
I follow my hero (Hector Sam), by turning my back on the goalkeeper to try and psyche him out. When the referee blows his whistle I spin round and shoot. Unfortunately I usually hit the corner flag!

Interests outside football?
I like nothing better that frightening the odd damsel in distress on my days off.

Love of your life
Sadly you don't come across that many female dragons these day – I blame it on St George!

Worst thing about mascot life...
In the summer it's like having your own private sauna, and I always seem to have my back to the action when a goal is scored!

Best thing about mascot life...
The reaction from the crowd and particularly the kids. They don't seem to mind my smelly fiery breath!

Thanks to: Wrexham FC, and Empics.

Chairboys in the Chilterns

It's our duty to point out that Bodger has a strong connection with the Metropolitan Police, the details of which we couldn't possibly disclose. So, a word of warning – If you're a visiting fan at Adams Park, be very careful what you call him!

'Who are ya?'
BODGER

What's in the name?
One of the club's greatest players, Tony Hoseman (Wycombe Wanderers 1963-78), had a nickname of bodger as he made chairs for one of the local furniture companies. He holds two club records with his 749 appearances and 416 goals.

Nickname
Ask the visiting fans!

What's your trademark?
Bodging! You can do it as a mascot as well as with wood! So I do lots of crazy things when I'm on the pitch – anything goes!

How do you take penalties?
I'm a blaster – it's the only way with the outrageously daft boots of mine.

Love of your life
I'm always on the look out for a Mrs Bodger. I came close a few seasons ago with the dancing girls during our FA Cup run to the semi-finals. They were only after my body though!

Best mate
Happy Harry of local rivals Luton is always leading me astray – good on him!

Highlights of your career...
Being sin-binned in a 'Mascots on Ice' game at the London Arena was one of my proudest moments and looks great on my CV! I had my hair done on Channel 4's programme *The Salon* in 2003 – Bodger is known for his fashion sense!

Best thing about mascot life...
Putting smiles on people's faces, doing community events, and believe it or not, being wrestled to the ground by the players. I'm much tougher than them but it's good for their confidence to think they can get one over me!

Thanks to: Wycombe Wanderers FC, Paul Dennis and Ken Payne.

Bodger in the swing of things at Adams Park...

YEOVIL
JOLLY GREEN GIANT

HARCHESTER UTD
THE DRAGON

Giant steps

The Jolly Green Giant was created in 2002 by manager Gary Johnson in the build-up to Yeovil Town FCs first FA Trophy final appearance. Since enjoying himself at the final the Giant has done a lot of charity events, including the town carnival – he can't fit on buses so he has to walk the entire circuit! Yeovil's nickname is actually the Glovers, but a mascot glove just wouldn't be very cuddly.

The idea of the Giant is based on Yeovil's reputation as non-League football's premier giant-killers. Now holding their own in the Football League, however, the Jolly Green Giant is up there to be knocked down as one of the big boys.

Thanks to: Yeovil Town FC, Shaun Small, and Nigel Andrews (photo).

Deep in the wildwood

Legend has it that back in the middle ages, when Harchester was mainly covered in woodland, a purple dragon the size of a giant oak tree appeared after being disturbed by a group of boys. The boys were playing what we now know as football – kicking a pig's bladder around a woodland clearing. To the boys' horror, the fire-breathing monster raced towards them… but instead of attacking them it took up the pig's bladder and swallowed it whole. The boys gazed in awe as the dragon then disappeared back into the midst of the trees. Despite repeated visits to the site, the dragon was never seen again. The tale, however, became legendary amongst the local people.

When the original club chairman Harry Howell set up Harchester United in 1906, he honoured the memory of the dragon by giving the original stadium a nickname 'The Dragon's Lair'. Soon the purple dragon came to life as the club mascot, and he now helps the fans roar on the club to Premiership success. But be careful he doesn't eat the ball…

Harchester United and the Dragon can be seen throughout much of the year on Sky TV's *DreamTeam*.

Thanks to: Ellen Taylor and Angela Hallam.

THEY MAY NOT BE ON THE BIG STAGE, BUT NON-LEAGUE MASCOTS CAN BE A STAR ACT. HERE'S A SELECTION OF TOP FURBALLS WHO ARE CERTAINLY NOT BOTTOM OF THE PILE.

A fit again Billy is up and running, and alas, cheating. Lingfield Racecourse disqualified him at the 2004 mascots' furlong for feigning injury to get bags of sympathy and a head start.

Thanks to: www.kipax.com, Ian Leech, Halifax Town. *Exeter Express & Echo*, and Exeter City FC (photos) Colin Deadman and Chris Richardson, *Heartland Evening News*, Aldershot News, Weymouth Town and Tim Davis, Woking FC, Steve Watkins and Stevenage Borough, Carlisle Utd FC, Lofus Brown of Cumbrian Newspapers Ltd.

BURTON ALBION
BILLY BREWER

Burton upon Trent has a long tradition of making fine beers. Everywhere you look there are breweries, and the well-rounded Billy Brewer, mascot of Burton Albion, enjoys a life dedicated to sampling their products. But on matchdays at Eton Park, things are different. He can't be tempted with a tipple – he's got kids to welcome and pranks to perform.

Billy is well known in non-League footy. He runs amok at many grounds and he's been asked to train new mascots at other clubs. He's certainly a celeb in home town Burton – a local burger bar has done a promotion based on his famous waistline, a 'Billy Brewer Happy Meal'. Perhaps Billy will do a sponsored diet next, especially as he started streaking right down to his padding in 2003/04. The beer-swilling star was filmed for three days in the build up to the 2003 Mascot Grand National, and replica Billy toys sell in several rival clubs' shops. Billy's groupies are not just in Burton…

CREATURES
FROM THE DEPTHS

EXETER CITY
ALEX AND ATHENA

So Exeter City are 'The Grecians', but why? The best guess is that their St James' Park ground was in an area settled by a Greek community in the late 1800s. But the Exeter town and club crest shows two flying horses – and Pegasus the flying horse comes from Greek mythology. Whatever the origins, the Greek gods have now descended upon Exeter to act out their legends – Alex the Greek is a gallant and dashing gladiator, protected by special armour used in the hit movie Gladiator, so he has a lot to live up to.

In 2002 the gods blessed Alex with a partner, Athena – Goddess of the City. Athena in mythology is protector of heroes and warriors. Athena soon took the media by storm, appearing on TV's Soccer AM, in the News of the World and in the Star on Sunday. She also stole the show at the 2002 Mascot Grand National, which she bravely tackled in her high heels.

Athena helps distract other mascots during Alex's penalty shoot-outs, and other teams' players when Exeter take the field. She gets fan mail every week, including from inmates who write in for her pictures.

HALIFAX TOWN
FREDDY FOX

Frederick Fox, as he likes to be known, joined the Halifax set up in 1996 – the rebuilding of the club's stadium disturbed his den, and it was simpler to move in at the Shay. He gives out sweets, does spectacular skidding dives, and drives a Foxhole Vectra.

When Freddy gets caught short he makes for the opposition goalpost and cocks his leg. He tried this on a Rochdale post once, but Desmond the Dragon took offence. Instead of singeing Freddy's whiskers, Desmond cuffed him with a scaly paw. Freddy stood up for himself and, true to form, the tussle was all over the papers. When police searched for Freddy after the game they were told to look for a chap with long whiskers, big pointy ears and a bruise on his nose.

KINGSTONIAN
FLAXEN THE SAXON

Seven Saxon kings were crowned at Kingston in Surrey between AD 900 and 1016. Of these, Aethelstan reigned for fifteen years as undisputed king of England. A model of him is even in Kingston Museum, where you can see his famous flaxen hair. The Coronation Stone can still be found outside the Guildhall as a reminder of Kingston's Saxon times. But real live history can be found inside the football club at Kingsmeadow, where the flaxen-haired king was reawakened for an FA Trophy final.

The link between football and combat is surprisingly strong in the town – there is a Saxon custom of decapitating a beaten opponent in battle to use his head as a football. Kingston's regiment, the East Surrey's, have a tradition of kicking a football on the field of battle, and Kingson was once famed for its Shrove Tuesday street football until it was banned in 1867 for its danger to people's property and limbs. It puts the rough and tumble of furry mascots into perspective…

TELFORD UTD/AFC TELFORD
BENNY BUCK

Benny spends pre-match warming up with the young match-day mascots and at half-time he dishes out fruit drops and humbugs. Due to Benny's limited vision he is unable to see many of the likely recipients of his goodies, but if they shout a quick 'Wahay!' Benny will seek them out and lob them a mojo!

Few mascots can speak, but it's good to have a one-word vocabulary at least, and Benny can wimper it or roar it, depending on his mood. Mascot events across the country wouldn't be the same without Benny's unmistakable and unmissable 'Wahay!'

As this book went to press, Telford United went into liquidation, and a downbeat Benny gave us the following interview:

'A new club, AFC Telford United, have been formed and will play in the Northern Premier league Division One, three leagues below the Conference. That's tough, but not half as tough as going out of existence altogether. I reckon I must now be near enough the lowest-ranking mascot in the country. Now that's something to crow about eh?'

CREATURES
FROM THE DEPTHS

ALDERSHOT TOWN
THE PHEONIX

CARLISLE
FOXY

FARNBOROUGH TOWN
BORO BUG

MERTHYR TYDFIL
SHAGGY THE SHEEP

NUNEATON BOROUGH
BREWNO THE BEAR

STEVENAGE BOROUGH
BORO BEAR

WEYMOUTH TOWN
TERRA-BULL

WOKING TOWN
'KC' THE KINGFILED CAT

YORK CITY
YORKIE THE LION

The Furry Phenomenon

York City has of late been a club in crisis – twice being on the verge of extinction since 2001. Amidst the chaos, Yorkie the Lion has been a courageous leader in both rescue acts, raising money against the closure deadlines and helping form the Supporters' Trust. He has fought for what he believes in – a club that is owned by the people of York for their own community. Away from Supporters' Trust duties, Yorkie is a rascal, a comic, and a charmer – never far from the centre of action, his passion for the club is infectious. Viking spirit lives on in York!

'Who are ya?'
YORKIE THE LION

What's in the name?
There are lions on the city crest, so I simply had to be a lion – well I could have been two, so I make up for it! My name is based on the club itself and our sponsor, 'Nestle Yorkie'.

Nickname
The Furry Phenomenon!

What's your trademark?
Well, aside from my dashing good looks, I have several moves that make the ladies go wild! Can't reveal the secrets though…

How do you take penalties?
I aim for the crossbar a lot, as mascot penalties are for laughs, not points. I also like to see how high I can get the ball over the bar from such a short distance – I've cleared the stands several times in my career!

Grand National finishing position?
Erm, last! Actually, it's far more fun loitering at the back – I could tell a few tales!

How will you improve next year?
I won't! My personal trainers at the club have strongly advised me to avoid curry, jungle juice and women – the three things the Furry Phenomenon can't live without. Plus my hectic celebrity lifestyle and demanding schedule simply leave me with very little time to worry about such petty things as physical fitness!

Interests outside football?
My VIP lifestyle dominates my spare time. I enjoy socialising with my many famous female companions while drinking and dining around Yorkshire's finest establishments.

Love of your life
Unfortunately I'm not at liberty to discuss my love life as my agent has warned that female interest may decrease if I marry. However the tabloids have linked me with various names in the past.

Favourite food
Curry and jungle juice – breakfast of champions and favourite of many a mascot night out.

Who do you need to get even with?
Stewards who have tried to stop my antics – don't they know who I am?

Evening Press   Evening Press

In the community
I roar on various charities and schools around York – all part of a loyal lion's duty.

Worst thing about mascot life...
All the female attention – it gets a bit much at times!

Best thing about mascot life...
All the female attention – can't get enough of it!

Word on the street about you...
'The best and cutest mascot!' –
Lelani, *The Sun* model and every male mascot's favourite lovely lady.

YORKIE'S SCRAPBOOK
Highlights from a photo album found in Yorkie's Den...

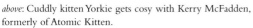

above: Cuddly kitten Yorkie gets cosy with Kerry McFadden, formerly of Atomic Kitten.

right, top to bottom: Yorkie with TV comic duo Ant & Dec as the mascots star on *Slap Bang* in June 2001.

Soccer AM cancelled! Yorkie makes off with Helen Chamberlin at her home territory – Torquay United's Plainmoor.

Soap star! *Coronation Street's* Vera Duckworth falls for Yorkie's charm during a visit to Bootham Crescent in 2000.

Manly advice – Yorkie and Man Utd's Fred discuss chat-up lines.

YORK CITY
YORKIE THE LION

THE YORKIE DIARIES...

It can be tricky getting a booking in Yorkie's diary, such is the pressure on the celebrity lion. Here's a snapshot of what he gets up to.

June 1st 2000
Even as a one-year-old, Yorkie is already a star in home town York – The Disney Channel Roadshow comes to the city, and Yorkie is invited along as a VIP guest and York ambassador. He later appears on stage alongside pop sensations Atomic Kitten.

December 1st 2000
The Monk's Cross Shopping Park in York holds its first Christmas lights show. Yorkie appears among the star-studded cast, including Craig from *Big Brother* One.

June 16th 2001
Alongside 50 of his closest furry friends, Yorkie appears live on Ant & Dec's *Slap Bang* prime-time TV show.

August 27th 2001
To raise money for a local charity, Yorkie agrees to be the first lion in history to perform a bungee jump. The brave lion made the leap from a 170ft platform in front of 2,000 amazed onlookers!

Yorkie Scargill forms the NUM – a National Union of Mascots to defend the rights of mascots!

Moonchester finds a Wheelie Bin is the best fit for Yorkie at Rockingham's 2003 Mascots on Wheels race.

December 2001

After details of a possible Professional Foootballers' Association strike are announced, Yorkie forms the NUM (the National Union of Mascots) to promote the rights of mascots. The mascots themselves threaten a strike and Yorkie's union work is featured in the *York Evening Press*. The local newspaper article sparks controversy and the story makes the national newspapers and TV.

December 2001–January 2002

After news breaks that York City FC is in danger of folding, the fans form a Supporters' Trust and use Yorkie as a figurehead. After playing a central role in developing the trust, Yorkie leads a 1,000 – strong march through the city before York's home game with Torquay on 12 January.

May 2004

Yorkie launches a photo exhibition of mascots at the Impressions Gallery, York. The event gives a lift to Yorkie, who is otherwise deflated by York City's relegation from the Football League.

Kirsten Gilies, Board member of the Supporter's Trust sums up their passion for Yorkie, 'He's king in the York City jungle – Yorkie, we salute you!'

The saga continues…

Thanks to: *Yorkshire Evening Press*, Andrew Leathley, Alex Bedingham, Steve Ovenden, Kirsten Gillies, and Sophie McGill.

Cultured creatures – Yorkie and his pals open the 2004 Mascots' exhibition in York.

YORK CITY
YORKIE THE LION

right: 'Save York City' front cover of paper

Shoulder to shoulder – Man City's Moonchester and Bradford's Lenny City Gent, and the Pie, visit Yorkie to promote the York City Supporters' Trust at York's Fans United day in 2002.

SCOTLAND'S
BEASTIE BOYS

All the way from China, the two pandas are now stars in their community as they promote Ayr United and help the junior supporters' club, Panda Pals.

Pandamonium led out Ayr United in the CIS Insurance Cup final against Rangers in March 2002. He appeared on BBC Scotland's *Offside* show with manager Gordon Dalziel and their host mascot, Jock the Cock, in the build up to the final. He was also bound and gagged and held to ransom by members of Ayr's South-East England Supporters' Club until they got the tickets they required for the 2002 Cup final.

Scotland's leading referee Hugh Dallas often meets the two critters at games, and recently said to Panda:
'I hate you as you never know what you're going to do next!' Ayr United player Paul Lovering has a superstition that he must shake Pandamonium's paw after he's run onto the pitch. He says 'It's just one of those things – I couldn't start a game without shaking hands with the Panda!'

Chaos made his debut at Hampden Park, live on Sky TV with his big brother Pandamonium, when Ayr played Celtic in the semi-final of the Scottish Cup in 2002. Manager Campbell Money once asked him to leave the dressing room before a match because 'It's 2.45 and it's Chaos anyway without you being here'.

Thanks to: William Barr OBE, Andy Downie, Ayr United (photo).

ABERDEEN
ANGUS THE BULL

The Aberdeen Angus breed of bull is world renowned for quality and strength, just like the football team! Angus proudly promotes the vigour of his breed and his club at Aberdeen's Pittodrie Stadium.

'Bully', as he is otherwise known, was born in the third field on the right, north of Turriff, Aberdeenshire. He led his team out at Hampden at both cup finals in 2001, and he gets more requests for appearances than the players!

Angus is usually careful when he stampedes, but he once ran out of the tunnel and collided with a BBC cameraman!

Word on the street about Angus…

'A fine, upstanding citizen' – *AFC captain*

'A clumsy b******!' – *BBC cameraman*

'He's mad as a hatter – must be the BSE' – *AFC match-day announcer*

Thanks to: Malcolm Panton, Aberdeen FC (photo).

BERWICK RANGERS
BRADLEY THE BEAR

Bradley is a bear from England who, like his team, dares to play in Scotland. Berwick Rangers don't play in bright holiday shirts or use beach balls though!

Thanks to: Bob Foy (Bradley Bear photo).

CELTIC
HOOPY THE HOUND

Hoopy is an all action hero – he's performed live on stage in Stuttgart with star singer Bonnie Tyler, and at the 2003 UEFA Cup final he got stroked and petted by 200 Spanish dancers in Seville – wow! You can read all about him in his book: 'Hoopy's Adventures in Paradise'. It's mainly pictures, but the poor mutt finds it beyond his reading ability.

Hoopy has been enjoying much success at Celtic Park and has become an avid collector of scarves – 61 were thrown to him in the 2002 Premiership trophy celebrations. The Celtic players gather in a huddle before kick off, and Hoopy has been named after this ritual – he gets called the Huddle Hound.

In 2004 he lost a pancake race to his great rival Broxi Bear, but in 2002 Hoopy won the race that counts – the 'mascot dribble'. His prize was one of mascot proportions – a year's supply of lager. Sounds like he needs more space in those kennels!

Thanks to: Empics (photos), and Action Images (photo).

'Welcome to Celtic Park'.
Hoopy in between his two kennels…

DUNDEE
DEEWOK

DUNDEE UNITED
TERRY THE TERROR

Is he from *Star Wars* or from downtown Dundee? Deewok the Bear writes up his diaries on the club web site and is always a bundle of fun. He once got ticked off for toasting in the new year at a match – he was only drinking water, but the police thought it was something stronger! He's also dressed up and danced with the Dundee cheerleaders, the Dee Lites, but doesn't think he's got the legs for a career in dancing!

Don't be put off by Terry's fierce looks – he can be a charming as well as a ferocious lion, and his friend Tina keeps him in check at their Tannadice lair.

Thanks to: Rob Foy, Dundee FC, Dundee Utd, Empics.

Marching bear –
Deewok in step with the pipers at Dens Park.

Sammy came to East End Park in 1995. The giant bear has been described in Dunfermline as one of the town's most famous sons, and is the proud owner of 'Scotland's Number 1 Mascot' trophy, presented by BBC Scotland.

Sammy does a different mad-cap routine before every home match. In eight seasons he has only repeated one of them, as a special birthday request. He's impersonated Elvis and General Custer and the routines have ranged from the Diet Coke Break, to *The Full Monty*!

Sammy's Gang parties feature a Sammy Story, where children read aloud a tale about Sammy while he mimes the hilarious actions. Four of the stories have been published in *'The adventures of Sammy the Tammy'*.

When we asked Sammy to describe his most bizarre moments he picked out the following gems.

'I was the first mascot ever to be thrown in jail, after being arrested at the match for stealing the half-time draw cheque. Don't worry, it was a fundraising stunt for Children in Need, where supporters paid £1 each to decide whether to 'Bail Sammy out' or 'Throw away the key'. Thankfully, the fans took pity and agreed to let me out!'

'I was involved in the first ever transfer of a mascot. We held a press conference to say I was being transferred for free under the Bosman ruling, to Dutch club Vernuftig Foppen because the club couldn't afford to hold on to Scotland's number one mascot. There was a local outcry before the club eventually admitted that 'Vernuftig Foppen' is actually Dutch for 'Ingenious Hoax' and it was an April Fool's stunt!'

'I did the pre-wedding entertainment at the first wedding ceremony at Dens Park in front of a stand full of wedding guests. I performed to the sounds of Abba to the great delight of the assembled guests and the vicar! The happy couple insisted that I piped them onto the park with my legendary cardboard bagpipes!'

Finally, we leave it to the local *Dunfermline Press* newspaper to sum up their hero...

'Sammy the Tammy's pre-match routines seem to have spanned from the sublime to the surreal. From the high point of 'Jake the Peg' which was featured on TV's *Scotsport*, Sammy has gone for a bizarre choice of music and mime. On Monday night, a be-kilted Sammy brushed away to the classic tune 'My old man's a dustman', before pulling a series of objects from a black binliner. In addition to a wig – Chick Young's hair (ha ha) – he revealed a winning lottery ticket, a Teletubby and a Barbie doll. But why? Please can someone enlighten a bemused reporter or else send for the men in white coats to give our mascot a full ex-SAMMY-nation!'

Thanks to: Dunfermline Athletic.

ELGIN CITY
BRIGGSY THE BADGER

Black and white stripes most often make for magpie mascots in England, and pandas in Scotland. But Briggsy has a nocturnal existence as a badger. He likes the evening floodlights though, and shows up on Saturdays at his Borough Briggs home.

HAMILTON ACADEMICAL
HAMMY THE HAMSTER

Hammy is the lively pet mascot at the Accies' home at New Douglas Park. He's the biggest hamster in Britain – how would you fancy cleaning his cage out?

HEARTS
JOSH AND JEMMA

Josh and Jemma are the new kids at Tynecastle, now that Hearty Harry has left the Heart of Midlothian. The previous Hearty was once on TV giving cover to soccer star and pundit Ally McCoist – it was a different type of diving header for Ally!

INVERNESS C T
ANGUS THE STAG

Angus prefers Caley Thistle to the forests and moors of north Scotland. But it can be wild at the Caledonian Stadium too!

Thanks to: Elgin City FC, Northern Scott (Briggsy photo), *Hamilton Advertiser* (Hammy photo), Hearts FC (Josh and Jemma photo), and Empics (Angus photo).

KILMARNOCK
NUTZ

LIVINGSTON
LIVI LION

Originally from Nutbush, USA, Nutz is the only blue and white squirrel to be found in Britain. His markings are a perfect match for the Killie colours, so this friendly squirrel has settled in at Rugby Park.

As well as having very squeaky paws, Nutz claims two records amongst the mascots – the biggest tail and the longest handshake. Best to avoid shaking his paw as he'll shake your arm off – squirrels don't let go easily, in case it's something to eat!

Back home, Nutz has a big family including brothers Cashew and Pistachio, sister Brazil, dad Filbert, and mum Hazel.

As well as hoarding nuts, squirrels like pinching and collecting things. Nutz is no different, and can often be seen scampering off with the match ball before kick-off at Rugby Park.

Thanks to: Kilmarnock FC, Eric Young, Joe Tanner, Ian Ferris, and SMG Newspapers.

Livi is one of the liveliest furballs in Scotland and often travels beyond his own jungle at the City Stadium. When not at his den he's quite a shopaholic, so watch out in the sales!

Nutz enjoys a friendly workout with Paisley Panda.

MORTON
CAPPIE THE CAT

The moggie at Cappielow Park was suggested and named by young Greenock Morton fans, and arrived on the scene in 2002. He's all stripes, claws and whiskers, and his ears glow in the dark!

MOTHERWELL
CLARET AND AMBER

Two bright bears bring the club colours to life at Fir Park. It's especially good to see Amber – Scotland's mascots could do with a few more women around the place. Mind you, she's already been rugby tackled by Sammy the Tammy, who gave her no quarter – those red boots won't stay clean for long!

Thanks to: Empics, Greenock Morton FC, and Motherwell FC.

PARTICK THISTLE
PEE TEE

RAITH ROVERS
ROARY ROVER

Pee Tee, the giant toucan, was hatched at a Partick Thistle 800 Club committee meeting. In case you hadn't spotted, his name comes from the club's initials, but his famous nickname, 'The Firhill Flyer', comes from a club legend – Johnny MacKenzie. PeeTee has been part of two consecutive promotion celebrations, so counts himself as a genuinely lucky mascot, having got his team to the top perch.

Toucans are mainly black of course, but with the Scottish climate, PeeTee has gone purple with the cold. Pee Tee came to national fame in 2002 when he played a star role with Nutz the Squirrel and Paisley Panda in the brilliant Little Lantern TV documentary *Close Encounters of the Furred Kind*. The program showed some of the trade secrets of a toucan, but didn't reveal the bill for his bird seed!

Roary came to Raith in 1996/97. He claims they were relegated from the Premier League because they wouldn't give him a game. He helps with the club's weekly lottery which is even named after him – Roary's Super Lotto.

Roary has the following to say about his dazzling career: 'I was once banned from attending a relegation decider at Alloa Athletic. They said it was because they thought I might start trouble, but I think it was because they were terrified that I might be playing!'

Thanks to: Jim Foy, Tony Fimister, Lawrence Bayliss, Raith Rovers Supporters Club.

Thanks to: Partick Thistle 800 Club, Junior Jags, SMG Newspapers.

On patrol at Ibrox… A bear called Broxi.

Thanks to: Action Images.

STENHOUSEMUIR
WILLIE THE WARRIOR

ST JOHNSTON
SUPER SAINTEE

Willie is sponsored by the club's Norwegian Supporters' Club. A dog once ran onto the pitch at Ochilview Park in pursuit of Willie. It grabbed Willie by the leg and wrestled the giant viking to the ground. She didn't sustain any injuries and feels sorry for the mutt for having sampled Viking flesh!

Thanks to: Stenhousemuir FC.

Contrary to popular belief, Saintee, the surreal giant at

McDiarmid Park, does not have a football stuffed up his jersey.

Thanks to: *Perthshire Advertiser.*

If the mascots are superheroes, what does that make

the artists and designers who bring them to life? How do they dream up the characters? How do they make them funky and cool, and give them attitude? They can make eyes blink, put fierce snarls on lions, create huge clumpy boots, and tailor a suit for a mascot's Sunday best. Britain has some of the world's top mascot makers. Here's a view from some of them to give us a glimpse behind the fabric, glue, and stitches.

Rainbow Productions

Rainbow Productions creates mascots for international sporting events, high profile clubs and small local teams, across the UK, Europe, and beyond. Rainbow has been the official mascot supplier to the last four major soccer tournaments – including the 2002 FIFA World Cup and Euro 2000 and 2004. Rainbow was

formed in the 1980s and has been overseen by managing director David Scott.

Rainbow is proud to have been involved in selling the modern-day concept of mascots to football clubs when pre-match entertainment was a challenge to clubs in the 1980s and the need to create a family atmosphere was greater than ever.

Rainbow is responsible for around 70% of the football

Wombling free…
Wandle Womble was created by Wimbledon-based Rainbow Productions. She then walked around the corner to take up residence at Wimbledon FC. Until her retirement at Selhurst Park in 2003 Wandle was a popular character at matches and at mascot events, linking Wimbledon FC with the famous television creatures who roam Wimbledon common.

mascots created in the UK. It provides a comprehensive training program for 'mascoteers' at football clubs, and it keeps an avid interest in appearances made by the characters – part of the satisfaction of creating mascots is seeing them in action. Rainbow staunchly champions the cause that 'mascots matter'!

Character Logistics

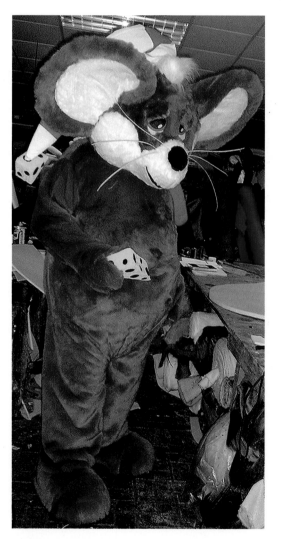

Character Logistics have been making mascots and characters since the late 1970s. Each character is created as a separate being, with love and attention to detail, in their workshop in Bognor Regis. All the characters are made individually, with no use of a mass-produced base, so each one is unique. Character Logistics are artists, sculptors and designers all in one. Hence, for example, Cyril the Swan, Jude the Cat, Whaddney the Robin, and H'Angus the Monkey are all individuals – as indeed they should be.

Angela Hallam
Angela is a designer and maker of costumes and all things weird. Her first animal costumes were for her ex-husband's rock band's video in 1982 (alas it was never released). She sold the costumes to a fancy dress shop and the owner asked her to make some more. Wolves and then Aston Villa heard of her work, and the rest is history!

Angela says the main issues in designing a mascot are that it reflects the image of the club, has humour and appeal, and can be worn and moved in easily and comfortably. Her various interests all come together in designing and making mascots. She's an artist, musician and writer, and is trained in theatre design. She's also involved in teaching mathematics, science, technology, and engineering. Maths, she says, is more important than you'd think in creating a mascot!

Costumes with Character

A giant mouse roams the studios of Character Logistics. Sedge the Fieldmouse is the resident rodent at Sedgefield Racecourse. Sedge's neighbour H'Angus rocked the political scene in 2002, clinching the Mayor's position in the Hartlepool election. Now it could be Sedge's turn to go one better in the next general election – and whose constituency is Sedgefield? None other than the Prime Minister's himself! Watch out Tony – the people of the North East like their mascots, and who'll get all the tactical votes?

Costumes with Character began as Situation Clothing in Manchester in 1986. It has a team of sixteen people creating flocks and herds of characters for sporting arenas across the world – their mascots bring enthusiasm, impact and fun wherever they go.

Sports characters are not just mascots, but essential team members. To prepare them for their challenge, Costumes with Character make sure they are well trained and in peak condition. Their creations include several of the north-west football and rugby club mascots, England cricket's Park Side Lions, Mad Ferret and Kit, who hosted the Commonwealth Games in the company's home town Manchester.

Thanks to: Rainbow Productions, Character Logistics, Angela Hallam, and Costumes with Character for information and photos.

Pranks, water fights, friendly sparring – it's all part of a mascot's act and what the fans expect. Good mascots go to the line of what's possible, but they don't cross it. They are entertainers – not thugs. They know their responsibilities. But on rare occasions the rough and tumble has gone too far – comedy has turned to tragedy. Such incidents are not forgotten. In front of thousands of people there's no hiding, and cameras are never far away.

The most legendary incident was the fairy tale which came to life – when three not-so-little pigs scrapped with Wolves' Wolfie at Bristol City in 1998. The pigs were visiting Ashton Gate that day, doing half-time penalties with Wolfie and promoting their company in the process. Suddenly the giant characters lost the plot – tempers frayed, and paws and trotters lashed out. Bristol City's own City Cat joined with stewards to keep the peace.

Hamster gets real – Angela Hallam's sketch design for Hamilton Academicals' Hammy the Hamster, together with the resulting real creature.

MEET YOUR MAKER
THE ANATOMY OF A MASCOT

right: Fur on the hills – Murmel the Winter Olympics mascot hurtles downhill at the Innsbruck games. Costumes with Character enjoyed the challenge of creating this fury bundle, who needed to be streamlined for the piste.

Bradford's Billy Bantam – a creation of Costumes with Character, who takes no responsibility for his actions.

MASCOTS BEHAVING BADLY

Referee Paul Taylor recalls he was having his half-time cuppa when a steward burst in his room, calling for help. 'What should I do, show them a red card?' said Taylor. He let the stewards drag the furious creatures apart. Supporters gazed in disbelief, and TV channels queued up for the footage. Bristol City and Wolves were none too pleased at the disgraced mascots, and took disciplinary action. As a sideshow to the main event, Wolves won the match 6-1.

The former Wolfie and three pigs were interviewed on television in 2003 – they re-lived the moment and were happy to make up. The bust-up at Ashton Gate is a vivid memory of mascots for most of us – but remember, the characters prefer not to knock each other's stuffing out!

Thanks to: *Bristol Evening Post* (photo), Guy Minter (illustration), Bristol City FC, and Paul Taylor.

Trotters, fists and paws: Wolfie and a pig clash in the famous bust-up at Bristol City's Ashton Gate in 1998. The other two pigs were soon at the scene.

YOUR COUNTRY NEEDS YOU

CREATURES AND THEIR CULTURES

Just like people, mascots reflect the traditions and fashions of their cultures. The different styles and colours of the mascots around the world add to the interest – so here's a few, at club and country level, from a few corners of the globe…

Thanks to: Dunfermline Press (Sammy photo), Empics (photos) Action Images (World Cup Willie photo). David Barber at the FA (World Cup Willie info).

Shimizu S Pulse of Japan

Japan's three-legged crows

The Nigeria Super Eagle

Poland's crow

Holland's lion.

Sammy the Tammy waves the flag for Scotland

Phoxy, of Dutch side PSV Eindhoven

Indi, of Spanish side Atletico Madrid

YOUR COUNTRY NEEDS YOU
CREATURES AND THEIR CULTURES

right: World Cup Willie – a vital part of England's 1966 World Cup triumph

below: England – three lions, or are they? The three lions on the Arms of England were first seen on the seal of Richard the Lion heart in 1194, but they may actually be leopards. In heraldry, when the big cat is shown walking forwards, looking full-faced at the viewer, with one paw raised, this is known as the 'passant guardant' position, and it's a leopard! There are no such doubts over the rampant lion on Scotland's emblem though!

below: Euro 2004 host – Portugal's Kinas warms up for the European Championship

CHADDY THE OWL
Oldham Athletic

When I started doing Chaddy in 1998 nobody saw much potential in mascots. Ours was a tatty old costume and I applied after seeing the 'job' advertised in the *Oldham Chronicle*. Everyone was telling me 'Don't do Chaddy – people keep saying get rid of Chaddy the Owl'. I soon turned it round, however, and within a few weeks the fans loved him.

After winning over the supporters to Chaddy, the club changed the head in 2000. Most people thought it was hideous, kids were frightened, and my own dog attacked me with it on! Luckily we were able to get sponsorship for a friendly-looking new costume and so the scary head's life was short.

Happy families
I saw Chaddy's potential straight away. Having a kid myself I knew that when your children are happy, you're happy, so I thought that supporters could bring their young kids to games and enjoy themselves even more. When I started, the number of Latics fans attending under the age of seven (who get in free) was about twenty. The number has now rocketed to two or three hundred. They may get in free but they are the supporters of the future and have merchandise bought for them, so the club still gains. The number of women attending matches has also gone up a lot over the last few years.

The Grand National – what a hoot!
I've become well known for my performances in the Huntingdon Mascots' Grand National. In 2002 I finally won the race, and by a long way. The Ladbrokes spokesman said 'When Chaddy took his head off, I half expected to see Colin Jackson in the costume'. I was 6/4 favourite at the course when the race started, but a lot of Oldham fans had backed me early at the crazy price of 40/1 and stood to win a lot of money. So there was a lot of weight on my shoulders as well as a giant head! Ladbrokes alone paid out over £30,000 on me.

Dodging the streaker
At the 2003 Grand National there were rumours circulating of Chaddy being snared during the race so others could take the crown. It turned out that a streaker was the main ploy to halt me, but I darted round the lovely lass and stayed upright to win again. The odds on Chaddy were short, so there were no betting scoops to be had this time. The race was also notable for the failed attempt by athlete Allyn Condon, who attracted big bets from those who knew his disguise of Sedge the Fieldmouse. But Sedge's boot came off at the first jump and he never recovered. Allyn Condon may have competed in the Olympic Games and won a Commonwealth 100m relay gold medal, but the Mascot Grand National was a step too far for him!

Thanks to all the publicity we got from the 2003 race win and Granada's plug about bringing a friend to watch

"I'm a celebrity...!" Chaddy is presented with the 2002 Mascot Grand National trophy by Catalina, model and star from the ITV series *'I'm a Celebrity Get Me Out of Here'*.

INSIDE OUT
LIFE AS A MASCOT

Chaddy's lap of honour, the crowd for the following Tuesday's game against Stockport was estimated to be 1,000 above the average, which is important money to a crisis club, and bigger support is attractive to potential investors. Amongst all the turmoil at the club it was great to see the smiles back on people's faces again. The fun continued at the next game with *The Sun* bringing two of its models for a photo call with Chaddy.

Staying put
In the early stages of doing Chaddy I received three final warning letters from Oldham Athletic's chief executive. One said 'It has been brought to my attention that you were mooning at the Cardiff City fans'.

Quite a few other clubs have tried to poach me to do their mascot. The pay at one club was over three times as much as the small fees I've been paid before Oldham's cash crisis, but I love the club and the Oldham fans and don't want to leave them.

Kevin Williams (AKA Chaddy the Owl)

PEE TEE
Partick Thistle

It is a joy and a privilege to have the role of PeeTee – The Firhill Flyer – and the emotions and rewards can easily be summed up by one phrase: 'making kids smile'. Smiles from the kids (and adults too) can, however, only be received if they are first given out. Even behind the mask, you must smile. If you don't, it will show in your body and you won't get the rewards. The hard part of the job is keeping a seven-foot, purple toucan in a one-bedroom flat, fitting him into the back of a car, taking him surreptitiously to the ground every second Saturday and passing kids who are his best pals but have no idea who you are. But it is all worth it for those smiles!

A Toucan's gotta do what a Toucan's gotta do…

Chester Studzinski (AKA PeeTee)

A tough life: The overworked Toucan chills out.

Saving energy – Chaddy takes it easy at his Boundary Park roost.

FLOYD THE BULLDOG
Charlton Athletic

I have always looked for opportunities to step out from the crowd and act the fool for the benefit of others and the sound of applause! So when the club gave me the chance to perform, and I prefer to call it performing, in front of a modest crowd at the Women's FA Cup semi-final, it felt like fame had arrived.

Mascot nerves
I remember being very nervous after changing into the suit for the first time, and then there was a massive sense of being alone with the head on. I became very conscious of my own breathing, and apprehensive at the restricted vision. Even walking was an effort, with the fear of falling, hitting and bumping into things.

Once Floyd and his friend Harvey the cat entered the pitch things became very different – I soon lost the sense of vulnerability and was caught up in the mascot magic! All of a sudden, looking into the faces of young children, you could see the belief in their eyes – that this great big furry creature was real! Then a sense of responsibility towards their notions of reality dawned upon me.

Canine canter: Floyd comes up on the rails at the 2002 Grand National.

Having not done this before, the learning curve was very steep, but ad-libbing through the rest of the day, Floyd and Harvey made many friends, young and old, who enjoyed our antics. Darren (my fellow mascot who was performing Harvey) got a bloody nose when he asked one of the players to 'tap' on his head because his cooling fan had stopped. The lady in question hit him with a punch a boxer would have been proud of, and the head's internal fan hit him on the bridge of the nose!

Mud bath!
Our first scheduled event was 'Mascot Mania', organised by Bolton Wanderers' Lofty the Lion and the Mayor of Bolton. It was an attempt at getting a record-breaking number of mascots and furry characters together. Staged at the Reebok Stadium, it was all for charity, with mascot football matches and other antics. Mascots had come from all types of sport and business, as well as TV heroes like Sooty and Sweep, and Fireman Sam. We were in the company of many seasoned semi-professional performers – it was time to look on and learn.

Being new on the scene, we felt like outsiders amongst the football mascots as the different events took place. By the time of the football match many mascots had drifted away, sodden from the bucketing rain. All that were left were the hardcore… Lofty the Lion was true to his name, keeping out of trouble during the game, and conveniently getting sent off early because he was sporting a pricey new costume. He had already changed once to keep pristine for the cameras while the rest of us got wet and muddy. Harvey had a wrestling match with the Notts County Magpies and ended up in a heap after falling over the advertising boards. I had been involved in several improvised scuffles, all of which the rain-drenched crowd had enjoyed. Lofty looked like a new pin though, so some of us decided to remedy the situation, and following the commemorative photo, we dumped him, new suit and all, into a large puddle, and rubbed muddy water in. This was my and Harvey's initiation – we had proved ourselves unruly and worthy!

Mascots, previously aloof, were now giving us tips on mascoting, and ideas on how to get laughs. We were told anecdotes from previous events, and studied the deportment and the exaggerated gestures of the experienced characters.

INSIDE OUT
LIFE AS A MASCOT

The wind in your face...

The group gathered at Bolton had some exceptional characters. Captain Blade from Sheffield United was one – his broad Yorkshire accent made him a target in the day's banter. While he was taking a break, some of the other mascots broke wind in his pirate's head which he'd left in the corridor. As he donned the costume head and walked out of the tunnel for the match all we could hear was a muffled 'You rotten b******s!"

A comic boot assist

If there's one thing to make the hairs stand up on the back of your neck it's 27,000 people cheering as you emerge from the players' tunnel. I was lucky enough to get that opportunity at Pride Park in August 2002. It was the Queen's jubilee celebration at Derby County – part of the Midlands stage of the Queen's tour of Britain. We were one of the warm-up acts for the colourful event, and once again it was a mascots' footy match.

Reebok mud! Bolton's Lofty is comforted after getting a dunking from Floyd at Mascot Mania 2002.

Waiting in the tunnel to be introduced was nerve-racking for an apprentice mascot, but then it happened… as we stepped onto the pitch the place erupted! My adrenalin surge allowed me to charge about for the whole game, and each time two or more mascots crashed into each other, another roar went up.

Near the opposition penalty area, I saw a massive elephant, Coventry's Sky Blue Sam, about to receive the ball. At full speed I hit him with a sliding tackle, which was followed by cheers from the crowd. But then a second, louder roar went up – what was it? Vision restricted, I rolled over to see Cyril the Swan doing a goal celebration! I had tackled the elephant, won the ball and pushed it into the path of Cyril who blasted home the only goal of the game. This was a high upon high!

Pulling in the crowds

It was at the Blue Peter Bikeathon where I began to realise the influence that mascots can have. Having set the event off, done the usual autograph signing, had pictures taken, and given the customary handshakes and cuddles, we noticed the stalls run by charities were not doing much business. Harvey and I went to the stalls to have a go, starting with the steam engine ride. Soon after they were inundated with passengers, and so were the other stalls we frequented. We had pulled in the crowds and helped the charities – great! Our final act of the day was to get onto the stage uninvited with a band doing impersonations of Mick Jagger. So there I was, exhausted and sweaty, lumbering in a mascot suit to the strains of 'Brown Sugar'!

The dark side…

There is a dark side to being a mascot, which I've learnt from doing public shows, and that is the inability to associate a mascot with a living organism (person or beast) by some older children, who take delight in inflicting pain. Fortunately this is a minority of children, but this element will crop up at nearly every event. Some youths at the Bikeathon thought it would be 'cool' to steal the mascot's head. Overheard by my wife, a group of them mused on the idea, but fortunately lots of young children surrounded me as I emerged from the marquee, thwarting the rogues who wanted to make off with Floyd's head as a trophy. It proves that mascots need their minders – you never know who might do something out of order, and especially out of your line of sight.

The run of your life

The last major event of the year for me was the Mascot Grand National held at Huntingdon. Yes, the hardcore mascots were there, on a blistering hot September day. This was an international event in which the mascots were paraded around, bets placed and a race run over shin-high hurdles, all for the NSPCC.

My son performed Harvey that day. At the opening of the Norwich Union Athletics Grand Prix he had run the mascots' 100 metres as Harvey in fifteen seconds, beating the rest of us by a distance. His odds at Huntingdon were very short, but the best he could do was sixth. I came twentieth as Floyd – enough mascots take it seriously to make for stiff competition. But the main part of the day was the chance to entertain the crowd of several thousand who had come to see mascots as well as horses.

Personality clash

Being Floyd or any mascot is not just wandering around in a furry suit as I first thought – you have to don the personality of the creature. I have coaxed, embarrassed and even frightened children to shake hands and cuddle the giant dog in front of them. I have seen tears turn to smiles with toddlers, and have given delight to people with disabilities. It's an experience I will never forget, and it's a rollercoaster of emotions, with tremendous personal rewards.

John Roberts (AKA Floyd the Bulldog)

INSIDE OUT
LIFE AS A MASCOT

HARVEY THE CAT
Charlton Athletic

The disabled children at the front of the stand make my match-day duties so special – a hug, a stroke of the hand, an autograph – you need to see the faces to appreciate what it means to these children. I am the loving, friendly cat, while Floyd, my partner-in-crime, is the naughty one, running off with the steward's baseball cap, pinching the football from the children who are match-day mascots, and waving to the cameraman to get on television!

You have to enjoy being with people to be a mascot – the girl before me is now working at a holiday camp with children and loves to act in the company's costume. She's gone from being a crafty, purring, cuddly cat to a massive, grizzly, cuddly bear! Her best times with Harvey were hospital visits and the shocked and delighted faces of not only the sick children but all the staff, many of whom were as keen on meeting and playing with Harvey as the kids.

Cool cat – Harvey limbers up before the Huntingdon Grand National.

Beckham's bad foot...
Before every game Floyd and I take part in the photo-shoot with the match officials, team captains and young mascots. In our game against Man United in 2003 I was asked to move in a bit for the photograph. As I sidled up to the Man United captain I accidentally (honest!) plonked my huge cat paw on top of David Beckham's bad foot. His injured metatarsal was a national talking point at the time, and I apologised profusely. He was really good about it – he put his arm around me, and told me not to worry!

Being a mascot is brilliant – you can escape into the character on a Saturday and be something or someone totally different – who wouldn't like to do that now and again?

Sue Gallop (AKA Harvey the Cat)

POACHER THE IMP
Lincoln City

I symbolise my club in the same way I think the real imp, a carving on Lincoln Cathedral, would have symbolised the club. I am mischievous, but not offensive, and am naughty but not rude. The fun can be taken out of some mascots by over-strict rules at the clubs they represent, but Lincoln give me a free rein, and I do not abuse that trust.

Pride and passion
There are many moments when it is an honour to be Poacher, but a couple stand out for me. The first was the closest I'll get to an England cap, as I attended an Under-21 game at Valley Parade (versus Italy), having been invited by Bradford City's mascot Lenny City Gent. Eight of us mascots lined up on the pitch near the players for the national anthems. I was so proud I almost burst. You can't get feelings like that in any other profession.
The second was our Division Two match against Man City a few years back. We lost 4-0, but before the game I ran out onto the Maine Road pitch to a crowd of 32,000 people. I didn't even know where our fans were, then from over in the left-hand corner I heard a roar of 'Red Army!'. Just knowing I'd triggered that – that I was the first Lincoln City figure the fans had seen in this intimidating stadium – sent goose bumps all over me.

Stand up and be counted

In the summer of 2002 Lincoln City was under a very real threat of extinction. We were in administration and it was doubtful whether we could kick off 2002/03. A rally was organised through the city, with fans marching and chanting to drum up support for the club. It was truly amazing as I took my place as Poacher at the head of the 2,000 passionate people. Our local MP Gillian Merron was there, there were TV crews, and other fans from as far as Man City and Rochdale. Lincoln City Football Club is a massive part of our local community, and judging by the response of the fans, and our emergence from administration, long will it remain so! During the march I was passed a bucket to collect cash. I was jogging along, getting carried away by the emotion, when I walked headlong into a bench on the side of the street. I couldn't actually see it, so I careered straight over it and the bucket of money flew everywhere. I spent three days nursing badly bruised shins and a deflated ego! When the chance arises I do what I can for the local community – school fêtes, a few kids' parties, charity football games – I've done it all. I'm proud of what I do, but it is part of the job and I'm sure any person in this role would do the same.

The highs and the lows

The biggest problem with mascot life is getting attacked by kids – it's only a minority of course. I've been punched, kicked, spat at and had parts of my costume ripped off. I've also suffered vandalism of the costume, which is heartbreaking. On a lighter note, I suppose a midweek LDV Vans game is a particular low point. Eight hundred supporters turn out to watch two reserve teams battle out a dour draw, and I have to try and lift the spirits of the fans. It's no mean feat!

Save the Imps! Poacher leads Lincoln fans through the city to protest at the failed ITV Digital deal and its affect on the club's future.

INSIDE OUT
LIFE AS A MASCOT

The best thing about being a mascot is representing my club. I was never a good footballer, and I never will be, but Lincoln City is in my blood. In no other form could I feature so prominently in the club's activities. When we are experiencing a high, I feel it as a fan as well as a mascot. To stand in front of the Stacey West Stand and hear the fans singing my name, or even singing any City chant will never lose its appeal to me. Before the players come out I am the only person on the field. When they come out, I can see the stands erupt into a volcano of noise and chanting, spewing a lava of ticker tape and balloons. To be able to stand where I do, and see all that, I believe makes me the luckiest Lincoln City fan alive.

The second-best thing is the feeling of doing something, or being someone. Everyone wants to talk about Lincoln City. Everyone wants to hear a mascot story or an amusing anecdote. Some might think that meeting celebs or players is the highlight, but for me it's meeting other Lincoln City fans – they're the heart of the club and that's what it's all about.

Wild thing: Poacher boogies to his 'Lincolnshire Poacher' theme tune.

No place to hide

At a match a few years ago the crowd reaction seemed somewhat saucier than usual. I was getting wolf whistled, and bombarded with all sorts of comments and suggestions. I was a bit upset, so I turned to walk away and stumbled over my shorts, which had not only come down, but now tripped me up in full view of the stands – there's no hiding for a clumsy, half-blind mascot!

Perhaps the funniest moment for me (but not at the time) was a match in 1999 against Burnley. I was suffering from flu, and had been bedridden and off work for three days. Come Saturday I dragged myself down to the ground, and did my usual routine as Poacher. Following the game I hauled myself back into bed, and was still there on Tuesday. I roused myself for my work on Wednesday as an accounting assistant. On arrival I was met at the gates by my boss, escorted into a side room and promptly fired. It turned out that the company I worked for had been the match-ball sponsors, watched the whole game from the executive boxes, and spotted me before and after my routine. I think I got my priorities spot on though!

Finally, how about this little exchange between myself and comedian Bradley Walsh when I met him when the mascots were on Ant and Dec's *Slap Bang* programme:

Bradley: Can I borrow some aftershave?
Me: No.
Me to Companion: Who was that cheeky git?
Companion: That's Bradley Walsh, he's a presenter.
Me: Bradley who?
Bradley: Bradley Walsh. You're the Lincoln City mascot. At least I know who you are!

Oh to be a star!

Gary Hutchinson (AKA Poacher the Imp)

BENNY BUCK
Telford United/AFC Telford

Benny Buck started life in 2000. His birth coincided with the development of Telford United's 'New Bucks Head' Stadium and the club turning professional (for only a year or so as it turned out). This new era includes a big effort to increase the support base of the club. Benny is one part of that strategy. Since United's return to the new stadium there has been a marked increase in the numbers of eight-to-fifteen-year-olds at games. I feel this is as a result of both better facilities at the ground and, to some degree, the Benny fun factor. With the club's change to AFC Telford and a fall to the Nortern Premier league division one, the challenge is now really on to keep the youngsters coming.

My vision is really poor and leaves me struggling at penalties or finding the right person to hand a sweet too – but perhaps that's part of Benny's make-up – the awkward, clumsy animal that people see and know as Benny Buck.

As well as dishing out sweets at half-time, Benny's trademark is a 'Wahay' noise – uttered regularly and in different tones. It's an adaptable sound, perfect for a mascot's communication, along with the body language. I find that now, even out of costume, as I wonder around the town centre someone invariably shouts a quick 'Wahay' across the donuts in Asda or the personal hygiene section of Boots… still it's nice to be noted for something – WAHAY!

Lez Dean (AKA Benny Buck)

St Buck's Ambulance – Benny stole the show at the 2003 'Mascots on Wheels' race at Rockingham Speedway.

INSIDE OUT
LIFE AS A MASCOT

RAMMIE
Derby County

I believe that mascots have a duty to entertain the supporters of all clubs, not just their own. Any of our activities may be in the public eye and so what we do has to be top notch. We must help people respect other club colours and we must not encourage the young to act disrespectfully towards people.

It is humbling to see a child fight an illness because of something I have said, and it is very rewarding to make a difference to sick children's lives by giving them goals to aim for, and I can help them meet players and lead the team out.

I have been doing Rammie for over thirteen years and I am out in the community every day, so people know me and immediately think of Derby County. Being a mascot is my job, my hobby and my life. I have been full-time since 1996 and maybe I am more Rammie than I am myself. Rammie is so called because Derby are nicknamed the Rams, but the other connection is with my surname – MottRAM… so it's 'Ram me'! I am the people's mascot and I am at their disposal 24/7.

Dean Mottram (AKA Rammie)

On patrol – Rammie helps with road safety awareness.

THE BATTLE OF THE MASCOTS
ELVIS GOES TO SHREWSBURY…

The very first 'Battle of the Mascots' match at Shrewsbury was memorable. It was on April Fool's Day 2001, arranged by Lenny the Lion, Mrs Lenny, and their good friends at Shrewsbury Town. Around fifteen mascots stayed at the hotel prior to the match. We were occupying a table in the bar while around us a birthday celebration was in full swing. Every ten minutes or so, Bradford's City Gent, living up to his reputation, would go around the tables showing tricks, blowing and modelling balloons, and giving them to the guests. The hotel staff didn't like the way he kept interrupting people, but they were actually lapping it up and even put money together for our beer pot!

Mayhem in middle England

After a curry and a drunken night out, the following morning was amazing. Every mascot was up at 9am for breakfast without hangovers. Our first call was a newly-opened cinema. There was a football film showing and they had a goal in the foyer to promote it. As you can imagine, the mascots were on for a quick game of footy. We pulled the goal into the middle of the foyer

Lurking under the covers – Wolfie and Wendy relax on the morning of the big match.

and used Cyril the Swan's massive oversize football. I remember laying the ball off to Cyril and he hoofed it. The ball looped high and smacked into the popcorn machine! We decided to play outside afterwards.

Next stop was a church to witness a christening. While the service was on we waited outside. After about ten minutes someone started to chant 'Jesus is our Leader, Jesus is our Leader, la la la'. Can you imagine about twenty mascots calling this out in a churchyard? We weren't taking the mickey, it's just what mascots do – have some (hopefully) harmless fun and generally be cheeky. Not surprisingly the vicar came out to have words with us and he was stunned at the gathering of furry critters before him! Photos were taken with the family after the christening, and we hope we left no lasting effects on the dear little baby!

Still craving for more antics, a couple of mascots then decided to play a prank by putting someone head-first in a wheelie bin. They picked on one of the locals – Telford United's Benny Buck. It certainly muffled his constant yell of 'Wahay' which is Benny's famous trademark, and known and copied throughout Telford. Benny took it well, and didn't even send on the bill for fixing his buckled antlers!

Fur flies

The match itself was terrific, with the two mascots' teams roared on by a crowd of 3,000 – more than come to watch Shrewsbury Town sometimes! The flesh-and-blood character Alex the Greek from Exeter City, and Swansea's Cyril both ran riot, scoring goals, creating others, and generally exploiting the dodgy defence and shambolic goalkeeping of my side. Around thirty mascots turned up, with many of us being shown a red card, but we nobbled the ref a couple of times to get our own back. Eventually the pressure of keeping charge of a mob of lawless beasts got to him and he went berserk – robbing players of the ball, going on a mazy run and banging in a goal! There were several mass bundles amongst the mascots, which the ref didn't dare deal with, and many of the characters feigned injury to get attention from the physio of the day – a nurse called 'Luscious Lisa', who rubbed us with her giant sponge! The match finished 8-3. I was on the losing side, and so didn't get my hands on the furry cup, but who cares. At least I scored in an official mascot game, although I was never credited with the goal, which still grates. There's talk of an England v. Scotland match next (who will Swansea's Cyril play for?). That will see serious fur flying!

Elvis J Eel (AKA The King)

INSIDE OUT
LIFE AS A MASCOT

The child within us
Mascot maker Angela Hallam writes...

We all need fantasy, escapism, something to believe in that isn't real – or is it? It's a comfort thing – like that special teddy who made us smile as a child. Mascots allow the child in us to still be active.

Those that wear the mascot can be someone or something else. They can act the fool, hug children, women – and men! Show off, dance, mime, do all the things they couldn't or wouldn't do without that second skin. I have known wearers who 'are' the characters they dress up as. I have worn Sky Blue Sam (Coventry) on various occasions, and felt a strangeness inside him. My own personality has become as one with what I know the public are seeing and I have waved and danced (I actually moonwalked in the centre of the pitch at half-time!) Sam could do that, but Angela Hallam couldn't. The crowd saw Sam, not me!

Reunited! Angela Hallam meets some of her creations – Sky Blue Sam, Beau Brummie, Baggie Bird and Warwickshire County Cricket Club's Hugo the Bear.

The signature of mascots

All football mascots matter to their home crowds. They entertain the children – tomorrow's senior fans. They flirt with the women, and joke with the men. Thousands of people see them every week. The sad thing for me as a designer and maker is that the reaction is so different from a fashion designer whose clothes are identified with their name: 'Oh look – a Vivienne Westwood, a Stella McCartney!' Despite their popularity, no one says 'Oh look, that's an Angela Hallam!' I am as well trained as a fashion designer and my products have wider mass appeal, but whoever asks me for my autograph?

My mascots matter to me – they are my children, my creations. They come back for cleaning and repair like prodigal sons and daughters, and are lovingly restored and sent back, or collected by their devoted wearers who love to discuss improvements and extra features. Friends and acquaintances look out for my mascots and collect cuttings or video clips. If a mascot does something wrong – has a fight for instance, some people assume it's one of mine and that somehow I am to blame for its conduct. This is the downside to publicity!

The warm glow

In the 1980s, football had a bad image – with too many thugs and fighting on the terraces. Well-mannered fans were scared to go. The clubs looked to America and saw mascots and the family image of sports such as American football, baseball and basketball. The modern generation of football mascot in the British Isles was born! That was when I started, with work for Wolves, Villa and Leicester – then it took off.

Now money is tight, wages at the top are high, priorities are changing. But can we risk letting the game slip into a hard, cold image again? A warm family feeling matters. The child in all of us matters. We must never lose the ability to have fun as well as watching 'serious' sport – the game should not be only about big business! I work for clubs in all divisions and for nearly all of them – mascots matter!

Angela Hallam

HARRY THE HARRIER
Kidderminster Harriers

A poem from Harry:

Come rain or shine, snow or summertime,
It gets boiling in my skin, but still I have to grin;
But back in the crowd, my red face chants out loud
With a sly knowing smile, I was Harry for a while...

Harry the Harrier

Thanks to: Peter Higby (Chaddy photo), Kirsty Anderson (PeeTee photo), Bolton Wanderers and Bolton Colour Lab (Lofty photo) Chris Vaughan (Poacher photos), Empics, Derby Evening Telegraph (Rammie photo), Southen Utd, Shrewsbury Town, Angela Hallam, Kidderminster Harriers, Kidderminster Shuttle/Times and News, Mathew Ashton.

Touchy-feely: Harry does a wing-tip charge with the Kidderminster fans.

A STAGGERING SIGHT

THE MASCOT GRAND NATIONAL

They have their Derby run at Chepstow, a charity hobble at Lingfield Park, and a race on wheels at Rockingham Speedway. They even played football on ice at the London Arena, and they do a three-legged stumble at Sedgefield. But the highlight of the mascots' year is the Grand National at Huntingdon. What's so special about this colourful scamper, and what gives the race its magic?

When Dazzler the Lion won the third Mascots' Grand National, his club, Rushden & Diamonds, had just won promotion to the Football League. Despite this landmark for the club, they got more publicity from Dazzler's win than anything in their history. There is a mass appeal for this weirdest of races – winning means you and your club are destined for fame.

The world is watching...

The media love the barmy spectacle of 100 characters staggering along a furlong and six little jumps at Huntingdon. The race is shown by TNN and other television networks across the world, it's a favourite item for many TV quiz programmes, and it easily made Channel 4's top 100 TV moments. The event typifies the 'mad dogs' spirit of the British.

Amidst the scrum of the race it can be anything but lighthearted for some of the critters. Southend's Elvis J Eel sent forty of the furballs tumbling at the start of the 2001 race, and Hartlepool's H'Angus the Monkey runs straight across the field from the off, to cause maximum mayhem, or maybe he's got a poor sense of direction! The Scottish mascots come to get one over the Auld Enemy, while certain mascots prefer the role of bouncer, to spot and 'interrupt' others taking it too seriously. But for nearly all entrants it is just for laughs, to raise funds for good causes, and to be part of this spectacular assembly of mascots.

A furry flutter

Ladbrokes take bets on the race to raise funds for charities like the NSPCC, but the chance of a bookie's payout has often made supporters and gatecrashing mascots forget about the fun side of it all. We can only guess what motivated Olympian Mathew Douglas to compete as Freddie the Fox, representing a fake charity, and surge to victory in the third Grand National. Realising they'd spoilt the party, his backers returned the winner's medal later that week, during which time payouts had been suspended. Second-placed Dazzler

was then awarded the title, and bets on the foxy man went to charity. In other years good money has been made by Watford supporters in Harry the Hornet's 2000 win, and by Oldham fans when they took advantage of initial long odds on Chaddy in 2002.

Victim of success?

The 2003 race was almost overshadowed by the efforts of a betting coup, with top athlete Allyn Condon, hidden in Sedge the Fieldmouse and a streaker running into the path of Chaddy. Sedge lost a boot, the streaker grabbed in vain, and Chaddy cruised home, spoiling the hopes of those who'd tried the long odds on Sedge. Perhaps it's a tribute to the event that tricks are played to outwit the bookies, and that newspapers want a piece of the action. In the process, the race has lost its innocence. A colourful scurry of mascots has become a scene of plotting and high drama.

Tail-end charlies

As well as the fame of winning, you get noticed for coming last. Following the carnage of fur, slumped in a sweaty mass at the finishing post, several creatures just saunter along to vie for last place – in 2002 Yorkie the Lion escorted Exeter's Athena across the line in an amicable tie (or was he just after a date?). But the most spectacular last place came in 2001 – not content with puffing his way over a furlong, Shrewsbury's Lenny the Lion romped around the entire circuit after passing the finishing post. He even held up the next horserace on the card – Huntingdon's official excuse to the Jockey Club for the delay was 'a lion on the course'!

Whose silly idea?

The race was the brainchild of Jim Allen, racecourse manager at Huntingdon at the time. He knew the appeal of mascots and reckoned a racecourse event would be something special. Having dreamt up the idea in a pub, he decided to put it quickly to the test. With just a month's preparation he attracted seventeen characters to a Huntingdon race day in September 1999 – the first Mascots' Grand National. The punters loved it, Beau Brummie lapped up the winner's bubbly, and the mascots spread the word. As the race grew year by year the sponsors, bookies, crowds and media all enjoyed the mascots' cavalry charge, and came back hungry for more. Jim is now welcoming mascots to his new base at Sedgefield racecourse, while Huntingdon carry on the good work he started as hosts of the epic day.

Race day – festival and frolic

Race day itself sees a carnival of mascots in the Parade Ring. Many are limbering up in their wonderfully awkward, oversize bodies, while Captain Canary is spinning cartwheels and Baggie Bird effortlessly pumping press-ups. Others are inflating their egos and enjoying the chance of glamour – posing with models and showing off for the cameras. As they get to the start, 'Fanfare for the Common Man' booms out of the speakers, a celebrity guest raises the flag, and the mass of creatures scramble along the turf – some are seeking glory, others just want to stay upright! The winner takes less than a minute to storm home, the stragglers take over five. Afterwards the exhausted racers can hardly struggle over to watch the winning ceremony, where camera crews are massing, and the top four showing off their medals.

It might be simpler to watch it on Sky or BBC's *Grandstand*, but nothing can beat the close-up riotous scene of a hundred furballs on the charge. The mascots are a race apart. So too is this event!

Grand National One...
1999 – WINNER: BEAU BRUMMIE

above: Chomping at the bit! Birmingham's Beau Brummie dips his head and his chops to become the first Grand National winner at the 1999 event.

They started it! A troupe of seventeen mascots staged the first Grand National in 1999, little knowing what they had set off. The line-up includes City Gent and Billy Bantam from Bradford, Sammy the Shrimp in his psychedelic phase, Captain and Camilla Canary, Pete the Eagle, Deepdale Duck, and, in the centre, Cardiff's Bartley the Bluebird (now RIP).

A STAGGERING SIGHT

THE MASCOT GRAND NATIONAL

Grand National Two...
2000 – WINNER: HARRY THE HORNET

Getting cosy… Forty-nine creatures visited Huntingdon for the second Grand National. Critters here include, from the left, Sammy the Stag, Tommy T TrewBlu, Kingsley, Huntingdon's own Hugo the Hound, Flash the Falcon, Rockin' Robin, Eddie the Eagle (Essex CCC), and Yorkie.

Grand National Three...
2001 – WINNER: DAZZLER THE LION

2001, and who's this? Freddie the Fox, or an international athlete wearing spikes? The Olympic hurdler Matthew Douglas shows no mercy in accelerating to the line.

A STAGGERING SIGHT
THE MASCOT GRAND NATIONAL

Grand National Four...
2002 – WINNER: CHADDY THE OWL

A sweaty pile – Mascots slump to their paws and webbed feet at the 2002 finish.

Victory at last! After several near misses Chaddy celebrates at the 2002 race.

Stampede! The mascots come up on the rails at the 2002 Grand National. Those in view include (from the left) Mighty Mariner, Sammy the Shrimp, Ollie the Ox, Harvey the Cat, Marvin the Moose, and Thunderbug from Canada. The dark horse on the rails grabbed third place, and is trained by the race originator, Jim Allen.

Grand National Five...
2003 – WINNER: CHADDY THE OWL

Loitering with intent: Team Sedgefield – Previous years' Grand Nationals had traces of skulduggery, but at the 2003 race it was rife, as Team Sedgefield's characters left their calling card...

Thanks to: Peter Higby, Rob Howarth (Alban Donohoe Picture Service), Watford FC, Rushden and Diamonds FC, Huntingdon Racecourse, and especially to Jim Allen.

Marauding pirate – Sheffield United's Captain Blade amongst the leading pack.

Not a teddy bears' picnic – The gathering in 2001 grows to
over 90, and makes the Guinness Book of Records.